STRANGERS
No More

One Family's
Exceptional Journey
from Christianity
to Judaism

Shlomo Ben Avraham Brunell

gefen גפן
publishing house בית הוצאה לאור גפן
JERUSALEM ♦ NEW YORK

Copyright © Gefen Publishing House
Jerusalem 2005 / 5765

Typesetting: Jerusalem Typesetting
Cover Design: S. Kim Glassman, Jerusalem

ISBN 965-299-304-0

1   3   5   7   9   8   6   4   2

Gefen Publishing House
6 Hatzvi Street, Jerusalem 94386, Israel
972-2-538-0247 • orders@gefenpublishing.com

Gefen Books
600 Broadway, Lynbrook, NY 11563, USA
1-800-477-5257 • orders@gefenpublishing.com

www.israelbooks.com

Printed in Israel

Send for our free catalogue

Dedication

THIS BOOK IS dedicated to my dear wife, my best friend and critic, the love of my youth, the woman of valor, Runa who became Ruth.

And to our much-loved daughters: Linda (Lea), Sara (Rivka), Karolin (Yardena) and Josefin (Yudith), you make us so proud because you joined us in our double *aliyah* – our journey to Judaism and our emigration to Israel. May Hashem bless you with joy and fulfillment in His Land.

With Love,
Shlomo

Acknowledgements

It GIVES ME great pleasure to acknowledge a number of people who impacted, in one way or another, on the decisions that lead to the publication of this book.

I recall Ed Frank picking me up for my first job in Israel, and upon hearing our story, he instantly told me to write a book. Ed was an acquaintance at the Absorption Center, where we were staying. Every afternoon, for a few hours, I would pack first-aid kits in Ed's warehouse. It was then that the seed was planted, and further grew when, later on, I was asked by R. Tzvi Koren, a community rabbi and teacher, to lecture in Kinor David, a new Orthodox congregation, in Ra'anana. After continuous encouragement, and many more speaking engagements, I began to seriously consider the prospect of publishing our story. To all of you who pushed me to write – including Emunah activists in Herzliya and Jerusalem, the AMIT organization in Tel Aviv, and the Young Israel in Netanya – I thank you, because the process of writing my story has been invaluable. And today I am even more convinced than ever that I did the right thing when I decided to leave the Church, convert to Judaism, and move to Israel with my family.

I am happy to have been accepted by Gefen Publishing House in Jerusalem. It has been a pleasure working with the publisher Mr. Ilan Greenfield and the staff at Gefen. Thank you for believing in me, for showing your trust in the vision and importance of making *aliyah* (the spiritual act of emigrating to Israel). And my thanks go to the "Old Man," Mr. Murray Greenfield, for his wise comments on the manuscript and for the brilliant editing work done by Sorelle Weinstein.

I thank Rabbi Tzvi Koren, who was eager to get his hands on the first draft of my manuscript, and I was as eager to receive his feedback in return. Thank you, R. Tzvi, for your guiding comments and for your blessing of love.

I extend my sincere appreciation to Mr. and Mrs. Herb, and Barbara Greenberg, for the time they dedicated to carefully reading the manuscript. They made *aliyah* from New York, where they, for decades, had been active in many sectors of Jewish life, including educating Jews on the importance of *Eretz Yisrael* (Land of Israel) and *aliyah*. Your perspective and experience was very valuable in giving the story a presentable structure.

To my *hevruta* (learning partner) and mentor for the last two years, Rabbi Yitzhak Fischer – thank you for your sincere and encouraging comments on the manuscript. I appreciate your knowledge and straightforwardness. It's a privilege knowing you; I feel honored by your confidence in me. Ruth also extends a word of gratitude to her friend and learning partner in Torah study, Bernice Mandelbaum, who so generously has given of her time to teach and inspire.

I express my heartfelt thanks to so many of you in our caring *Kehilla* (community) and to our large circle of friends in Ra'anana, for the support you gave both in words and in action. Your friendly question: "How is your book coming along?" helped me in my writing, when often the only time available to me was the early hours of the morning before morning prayers in the *shul* (congregation) next door, before beginning the day's work.

I also want to acknowledge the part played by my wife Ruth. Her role is much more than that of an adviser or critic. Obviously this book is as much her story as it is mine. When it comes to writing the story she is also my best supporter. I am sure I missed many opportunities to give her a helping hand at home when my strength and my time were dedicated to writing. Still, she was supportive, the way she always is – independent, strong, and loyal, always willing to do more than her share.

Thank you all!

Shlomo

B"H

A Blessing of Love

To our beloved and honored Ruth and Shlomo,

It is the greatest privilege for us to see you come into *shul* and to daven together with you.

Thank you for being a constant inspiration in the Shabbat service and in the *tefilla* of our community.

May Hashem bless you with many happy and holy years together with all of Israel.

HaRav Tzvi Koren
Kehillat Kinor David
Ra'anana

Contents

Introduction

LEAVING THE CHURCH in 1990 opened up a new reality for me. I was no longer a registered member of a Christian congregation, but I was not yet Jewish. I suddenly entered a life formally without a religion. Spiritually it was a very empty world. That was a difficult experience since religion and spirituality had been such an important part of my life and personality. But on the other hand, the spiritual vacuum allowed a genuine search that, up until now, had not been possible. I started the exploration and enjoyed the freedom. The odyssey in the spiritual "no-man's land" lasted a few years until our family found a haven in Judaism and *Eretz Yisrael*.

What I found did not seem completely new to me after all, since my previous religion, Christianity, was based upon Judaism, but had been changed and falsified. Now I became eager in my search. I was no longer content with substitutes – I wanted the real thing.

The rabbi in Helsinki, Michael Alony, guided my family and me in our first conversion to Judaism. This Orthodox conversion was not the only one for us, but it brought us to Israel. My wife and I both were filled with an urge to come and live in the land of the Jews. We wanted to enter Israel as Jews and our conversion in Helsinki made this possible. The dream of those few years came true when we made *aliyah* to Israel from Finland in 1996. The move to Israel gave us roots in a completely new setting. The branch connecting us to our old homeland was severed; we were now replanted in a land that hopefully will witness the flourishing of new offspring growing up as Jews.

Jewish *halacha* (law) is very strict on conversion – when we arrived in Israel, we found that our first conversion in Helsinki was not adequate, since our rabbi there was unknown, and therefore we had to go through the process once more. This process required years of learning for all of us. Being tested in front of a court of three rabbis is no tea party, but it was worth it. We had to undergo these tests a few times. Finally we were accepted, and my wife and I were married again. We found a congregation, a community of friends. This was our *aliyah* to *Am Yisrael* – we became one with the Jewish Nation.

Life in Israel is incomparable to anything else. First of all we live as Jews in the only place we can call our own. This is the Jewish state where the national holidays are Jewish holidays. But all that glitters is not gold. In Israel we have to fight and struggle for our very existence, but at least here we are equipped with the means to do so. Threats emanate from inside Israel and from abroad. Is there a gas mask at hand in case of a missile attack? Suicide bombers strike at bus stations. Cellphones are frenetically ringing, everybody is calling to make sure their loved ones are safe. Life in Israel also means more expenditure than income, yet somehow you survive. It must be the land of miracles.

But we really and truly love it in Israel, simply because it is home. The sun is warm, the wine is good and whenever we feel like it, we can go up to Jerusalem. My wife and I have not been back to Finland since we arrived in Israel over seven years ago. Maybe we will visit one day, but Israel is our home. Finland represents our Egypt that we left for *Eretz Yisrael*.

This is not only my story. Through thick and thin, our family has stayed together. All six of us converted, twice. We are all still here. With no regrets. This is our *aliyah* to *Eretz Yisrael*, our settling in the Land of Israel. I am leaving this book, my personal account, as a document, a legacy to my children and, with God's blessing, their children. Our four daughters have been completely involved in this story all along the way. They were young when we moved from our home in Finland to Australia, started school in a new language and had to adjust to a different environment. Back in Finland it began all over again with new schools, new friends and new languages, this time Swedish and Finnish. Without doubt, moving to Israel was the most difficult of all the moves. Sometimes I feel anxious just thinking about how much we have put them through.

Young people are very adaptable, and they certainly learn from their experiences, but my hope and prayer is that we did not make their early years too hard with the many moves and difficult decisions. When we left the Church they followed automatically, because of their young age. Still, for them it meant staying out of confirmation class, when all their classmates attended the Church learning program. Later on, during our conversion in Helsinki, the girls were old enough, although just in their teens, to accept on their own the new faith and sign a statement declaring their readiness to live a Jewish life and bring up their children in the Jewish faith.

As the statement reads: "If I shall be blessed with male children, I promise to have them brought into the Covenant of Abraham. I further promise to bring up all the children with whom God shall bless me in loyalty to Jewish beliefs and practices and in faithfulness to Jewish hopes and the Jewish way of life."

My wife Runa, who became Ruth, followed me closely in every aspect of my religious development, and never hesitated about any of our life-changing decisions. We want to see the continuation of our faith in our children. Our conversion is a commitment for life and for generations to come. I want my children to know how privileged I am to have had a chance to gain membership into the Family of Israel. It came with a price, but it is a privilege, not a sacrifice. My prayer is to live a life worthy of the sacred fellowship that we have been privileged to join.

This is a very personal story. It flows from the deepest levels of my being and as such, perhaps should be hidden from the world. But like a string on an instrument, when it begins to vibrate, it creates sound waves whose immediate effect can be heard and even seen. So it is with the vibrations of my life – they touched my environment resulting in far-reaching decisions that affected my family, my work, and my future. My faith could not be hidden. It came out into the open, to the agony of those who disagreed, to provide comfort and inspiration to those in a similar situation, or to those who can relate to my questions. Allow me, as a stranger accepted into the family of Israel, to remind the Jewish people how precious is the gift that God gave, when He invested in us His Holy Torah and entrusted us with the beautiful Shabbat. Another gift God gave to His people is *Eretz Yisrael*. I am lucky to live in this land and I want to show more people the importance of making *aliyah*, to settle in the land of Israel.

Sharing my personal story with a broad public has a purpose. Knowing one's own identity is a human right, even a necessity. The search for it, I found, is closely connected to religiosity. We are what we believe, and if we don't know what to believe, we are like a grain of sand on the beach, lost in the multitude of pluralism.

It is all too easy nowadays to lose oneself in traditions and rituals. But sooner or later, there will come a time for soul-searching, a time to find meaning in the ritual and the story behind tradition. Lost souls must find their way home. I want to feel alive and I want my soul to find its proper place. My story is a search for the identity of my soul. Therefore I direct my thoughts to the Giver of life, to the One Who placed my soul within me.

This book reveals a long journey, the starting point being the world of Christianity, in which I served as a minister in a Lutheran Church, and the destination point being Judaism. It could also be described as a search for the God whom I knew from the Tanach (the Hebrew word for Bible, Tanach is an acronym of the words Torah [Pentateuch], Nevi'im [Prophets] and Ketuvim [Writings]), but who still seemed so far away.

My life as a Christian minister was filled with memorable experiences. I will share some of them in this book. My time in the Church also gave me work experience in another continent. Born under the Northern Star in the cold country of Finland, I sojourned with my family for five years under the Southern Cross in the land Down Under. Why wasn't it satisfying to be a Christian, or enough to be a respected minister with job opportunities around the globe? Why give up all these privileges for something so difficult and so different? Why leave an easy life in Finland or Australia to move to Israel? Finding an answer to these questions will take a lifetime, but I still want to share the decisions that I had to make, and the reasons behind them, because I believe that sharing my experience may help somebody realize or rediscover the preciousness and uniqueness of Judaism, and the importance of living in Israel. I am now proudly waving the Star of David as my flag.

Our generation has seen the deepest humiliation of the Jewish people, but we have also witnessed the success story of establishing a Jewish state. "For he that touches you touches the apple of his eye," says God (Zechariah 2:8). Painful experiences throughout history have made it difficult for so many to keep their faith. I want to convey my strong conviction that we are going to see a mighty revival of Jewish values. Amidst growing anti-Semitism we are not far from the time when nations – not only Jews – will realize that "out of Zion shall go forth Torah, and the word of the Lord from Yerushalayim" (Isaiah 2:3). Now we can look forward. The future will prove what Jews have always proclaimed, "Hear O Israel: The Lord our God, the Lord is one" (Deuteronomy 6:4).

The story of Ruth in the Tanach comes to mind when I relate the experiences of our family. Ruth is the famous convert in the Tanach. Her road to Judaism serves as a source for some of the major *halachot* regarding conversions. Ruth's life is also about commitment and dedication to the people of Israel and their God. The Book of Ruth is read during the synagogue service every Shavuot. There we learn that she became the great grandmother of King David, and therefore of our future Moshiach (Messiah). Her faith and conviction serve as a model for all of us. I wish to reiterate the famous statement by Ruth to her mother-in-law Naomi that echoes the deepest expression of my innermost faith and dedication to our new people: "Where you go, I will go and where you stay, I will stay. Your people will be my people and your God will be my God. Where you die I will die and there I will be buried" (Ruth 1:16–17). I will add another quotation from much earlier in the Tanach, and from another story, that of Joshua. This takes place at a critical moment when the people had to be reminded whom to serve. Towards the end of Joshua's lifetime he gathered the people at Shechem and presented them with two alternatives: Either you serve foreign gods or you serve Hashem. Then Joshua himself set the example when he expressed these words that I also want to make my own: "As for me and my house, we want to serve God" (Joshua 24:15).

These words are not only a statement but also a prayer for our children. May God keep you and safeguard you, may he protect you and bless you and instill in you the satisfaction of knowing who you are, so with pride and inspiration you can convey the legacy of our fathers to future generations.

Shlomo Ben Avraham Brunell
September 2004

ONE

From The Beginning – Our Early Years in Finland

MY CHILDHOOD HOME was quite religious. The atmosphere was warm and faith in God was taken for granted. Not only did my parents attend Church every Sunday, but I also recall my father sitting in the rocking chair in the kitchen, close to the stove where the fire was burning, during the early hours of the morning, reading the Bible. We lived in a small village outside the town of Karleby, or Kokkola in Finnish. I was the youngest of four and had two older brothers and one older sister. My grandparents had passed away before I was born. We spoke Swedish at home, the minority language of the Finns on the west coast of Finland, where our town was located, and in the south around the capital, Helsinki. The Finnish capital was far away, and we seldom traveled there. I made my first journey to Helsinki on a school trip when I was in the fifth grade. The 500-km (280-mile) trip was usually made by train since Karleby was on the coastal train line connecting Rovaniemi in the north to Helsinki in the south. Of six million Finns, about five percent speak Swedish as their mother tongue. Both Finnish and Swedish are official languages and the minority language has a guaranteed status by law.

Our home was built in 1949, only a few years before I was born. It was a modest two-story wooden house, painted red like most houses in the country. The boards around the windows were white. The yard was full of birch trees, which were a beautiful, lush green in the summer. When I think of my childhood home, I always envision the summer. In this beautiful garden, I learned to ride my bike, fell and scratched my knees, played football between the trees – we picked two trees and they were the goalposts.

I was often a one-man team, since my older brothers were too old to play with me. Sometimes my cousins or classmates came over. To see the winter picture, however, I have to search my memory – it does not come to me as readily. The winter was cold and frosty. The birches were bare. The only colors, besides the white snow, were our red house and the evergreen pine and spruce trees. The smoke rose slowly from the chimney straight towards the sky, signaling the coldness of the Finnish winter. This picture is also, in its own way, beautiful. But winter was not my favorite season.

Our part of Finland was flat as a frozen lake. There was only boring cross-country skiing, no exciting, fast downhill slopes. My cousins and I built a ski-jumping tower from a treetop in the forest behind my house. The tower was only fifteen meters (eight yards) high, but for the jumpers who had barely turned twelve it was high enough. I remember feeling scared. Here we were, building a ski-jumping tower, and when it was finished, I was too nervous to use it. Finally I summoned up the courage. Once I got the taste for it, I stayed until dark, or until my toes, ears, and nose were numb. Then it was my turn to sit next to the fire and warm up.

I would often attend church on Sundays with my parents. The church was some three kilometers away in the center of Karleby. It was a majestic, old, white-plastered stone building that dated back to the Middle Ages. The impressive walls seemed to me to be two meters thick. What the tower was not in height, it made up for in grandness, with its three large church bells inside, and, of course, the big cross that stood proudly at the top of the tower. This church seated 800 people. It was always full on the big holidays, such as Christmas and Easter, and at midsummer, when the confirmation service of the fifteen-year-olds who had attended confirmation class was celebrated.

In my youth, approximately one- to two-hundred churchgoers attended the regular Sunday service. In Karleby, as in all rural areas, over eighty percent of the population belonged to the Lutheran state church. The state average is slightly lower. The parish covering our geographical area of Karleby had 7,000 inhabitants. Serving this community were two full-time ministers and one cantor-organist, youth and social workers, and dozens of volunteers working as Sunday school teachers.

Israel and the Jews were held in high regard in our family, as well as in our community and Church. I cannot recall a single moment when in my home a negative comment was made about the People of the Book.

Without a doubt, I owe my early respect for the Jews to the teachings and examples of my God-fearing parents. They believed in the God of Israel and transmitted this faith to my older siblings and to me. Looking back, it was so free of conflict. The "Old Testament" was the sound and solid base, with Abraham, Moses, and the Ten Commandments, and as natural as the second floor of a two-story building was the so-called "New Testament."

I never questioned during that time why the Old and New Testaments were regarded in the way they were – these questions only came to me much later. My questions were still far from me when, as a boy, I would ride on the back of my brother's bike on the way to Sunday school. My oldest brother Borje used to be our Sunday school teacher. I was proud of him because he had a good singing voice and he made the Bible stories come alive. During the years when a teenager begins to contemplate his future, Borje took me along to the brass band recently established in our parish. I also joined the youth choir. In the band I played tenor horn and in the choir I sang bass. These activities in the Church kept me busy during my spare time for many years to come. Later on I felt limited in my social contacts, because in my teen years, I only ever mixed with the same youth group and the same churches – we sang and played in nearly every church and congregational hall throughout the country.

My strong involvement in Church activities during my high school years played an important role in my choice of university and field of study. My Latin teacher, Ms. Gadda, took it for granted that I would go to university to study theology. Sometimes her certainty would annoy me, arising in me the conviction that I would study anything but theology. I tried to think of viable alternatives, but in reality I could never make that leap in contemplating other professions. What about becoming an engineer or a dentist or, as I wanted most of all, a pilot? Airplanes have always fascinated me. Only a few kilometers from our home was a new domestic airport. As a young boy, I could see the old passenger DC-3 come in for landing, morning and evening, en route from Helsinki. Many years later, when the planes had been upgraded to DC-9 jets, I still ran to the window or out to the yard to catch a glimpse of the planes every time I heard their familiar sound.

Maybe those kinds of thoughts were too "high-flying" for the down-to-earth family that we were. We had a small farm with fields in front of the house and forests behind. In the barn there were cows and calves and one horse. Milking cows was closer to my reality than taking a seat in an airplane cockpit. Still, I have to admit that I was encouraged to study, especially by my father. In his opinion, anything was possible as long as I pursued an academic future. My father's positive attitude to life, and his belief that everyone could shape their own future if they only worked hard enough, was a great gift that has served me throughout my life. He himself regretted the fact that he did not continue his education, go to university, or follow another career besides farming.

My father had a special interest in forestry, a rather important field in Finland where the value of the vast forest landscape has earned it the nickname "green gold." Finland not only harvests and processes wood; the replanting of the harvested areas and cultivating the newly planted young forests demands knowledge of agricultural science. Despite tons of forest products being exported every day, the total volume of forest growing in Finland is increasing, not decreasing, thanks to the obligatory replanting scheme. My father taught this to me out of interest for the well-being of the soil he worked and knew so well. This was well before the green movement or ecological issues were high on any political agenda.

Our small town had a volunteer brigade of fire fighters and my dad was the proud fire chief. In the fire brigade, there was also a connection to preserving the forest. During the few hot summer days, lightning would strike and start a forest fire. Once there was a huge fire that threatened the whole village. It had been raging for several days and the exhausted firemen needed water, not only for the fire, but also to quench their terrible thirst.

My father was a young bachelor at the time, and he joined in to rescue the village from destruction. The fight continued for days. The girls from the nearby community did their share by bringing drinking water for the thirsty firemen. Along came a rather shy, young girl, perhaps in her late teens. She approached the men with her water bottle, and headed straight for the firefighter whom she felt needed her water the most. This man, some five years older, told us, his children, several decades later, how magical this water was. In the heat of the summer, this water did not kill the thirst, but rather lit another fire – the fire of love. The young girl named Linnea and the firefighter Runar married a couple of years later and began their family and their farm on the plot of land in the forest where they had met.

My father was quite a storyteller. When my wife and I were married, our wedding reception took place in the green garden of my home. My father paid tribute by telling us about the love ignited between him and my mother in that magical spot so many years earlier. I could see my mother's amusement. She continued to be the shy, but always supportive, partner to my father. She did not enjoy public appearances the way my father did. How could a farmer use his talents for public speaking? My father did not give speeches to herds of cows in the fields or to the tall pines standing erect in the forest. His personality made him a leader. In his world, which included the farming community, the forestry organizations and the Church, he was a member of several boards of directors. In many of them he served as chairman. These were the circles where he put his speaking talents to good use.

In her own way, my mother was active in her ladies' groups. Sometimes I wonder if my mother was really the shy girl she seemed, or was it just her manner in the shadow of my dominant father. Theirs was a good relationship. I remember only warmth and friendliness in my home. I was born after the Second World War, and saw very little of the real difficulties my parents faced during their lifetime.

Soon after the young couple had their first son, the Second World War began. Like most other Finnish men my father served five years in the army. For five cold winters he fought the Russians. Finland had no choice but to go to war with her neighbor, not because of sympathies with the Germans, but rather, had Finland not gone to war, she would have been invaded by the Russians. Later, towards the end of the war, Finland fought against the Germans when they tried to exploit Finnish territory for their warfare. The result was a devastating war in which the Nazis burned and destroyed much in their path, as the Finns chased them out of Lapland in the north. During the war my father was away from home, returning only on leave for short periods of time. My sister Berit was born before the war was over. My oldest siblings were married and had moved out of home before I was old enough to have any memories of that time. My brother closest to me in age, Birger, is "only" ten years older than me.

Borje took over the farm together with his wife Saga, and developed it into a modern, high-production enterprise, and, in turn, handed it down to their son Daniel. Borje's great interest – even greater than farming – was music. In his adult years he studied for his music diploma. He served in the local parish as cantor-organist for several years until his early death at the age of fifty-eight. My oldest brother was very devoted to his faith and was much loved among the parish members.

Berit married her teenage sweetheart Bengt and remained in our hometown. She studied accounting and worked at a local bank until her retirement. I remember as a young boy how we always expected them home for a Sunday afternoon visit. Being the only daughter, Berit was special to my mother, and the weekly visits were very important to her. My sister never once let our mother down.

I have some memories of my brother Birger living at home at the same time as me. But because of the age difference, I felt as if I were an only child. No sibling rivalry, no one to compete with, for better or for worse. By the time Birger married Benita, whom he met at college, the new trend for young Finnish couples was to move to Sweden. In our part of Finland, a minority of the population spoke Swedish. As far back as we could trace – to the seventeenth century – our family had lived in Finland, but the mother tongue was Swedish. Moving to Sweden was therefore not a drastic step. The neighboring country sometimes offered advantages for studies and work and the language for us was only a benefit. I believe for Birger, as for myself, that the Finnish language was never part of who we were. Birger and his wife moved to Uppsala where he studied theology and became an ordained minister in the Church of Sweden, a position he holds to this day. As a vicar in a large congregation, Birger is respected and admired both amongst his colleagues and the community at large.

As I matured, I regarded Christianity and practical Church life as a very important and natural part of life. I never felt any urges to rebel against this lifestyle. I had a spiritual need, and in my childhood and teenage years, that need was fulfilled.

I graduated from GSSL, Gamlakarleby Svenska Samlyceum in 1973 when I was twenty years old. The day before graduation I became engaged. My future wife Runa and I exchanged rings as a symbol of the promise we made to each other. We had met a few years earlier. She was a member of the youth choir and I was playing in the brass band. The choir and the band often went on tours together to perform in various parts of the country. I remember the first time that Runa and I spoke to each other. We were play-ing one evening in a church, and during the interval Runa came walking down the aisle with some girlfriends. When I encountered the girls, I only had eyes for her and said, "Hi, Runa." She blushed with shyness and was wondering why I said hi only to her. She found out and now the celebration for the graduation was combined with our engagement party. We were not the only couple to find each other in our circle of friends – our youth group consisted of a couple of hundred people and functioned very well as a matchmaking pool.

When I graduated from college and continued on to university, the only subject for me was theology. I have considered many times since my conversion to Judaism how easy life would have been if I had studied anything but religion. My wife and daughters have wondered the same thing, especially during the difficult years after leaving the Church. What is a degree in theology worth in a Lutheran country when you leave the ministry and the Church? Later on, after moving to Israel, I found myself asking the same question. Why did I make it so hard for us? My questions longed for an answer. I do not accept that my choices were wrong, nor will I accept there was no purpose in them. I am going to continue to look for the answer until I find it. I owe it to my wife and daughters. They have done more than just supported me, they have chosen to join me in all my difficult decisions.

TWO

My Entrance into Priesthood

THE YEAR WAS 1978. After five years at university, seventeen young theological students gathered in the old town of Borga to prepare for the ceremonial ordination into priesthood the following Sunday. The Medieval Dome stood majestically in the center of town, quietly signaling the influence and power of the Lutheran Church in Finland. By the foot of the Dome, the residence of the Bishop, a grand two-story mansion, was to house the reception on the eve of the big event.

The week had been busy with last-minute preparations. My formal graduation from university was complete. I had studied at Abo Akademi, the Swedish University of Turku, the cultural capital of Finland.The master's degree still felt warm in my hand. Now the Church was about to give its blessing to these young and eager students to start practicing what they had been studying for. Receiving a degree in theology does not, however, only qualify you to become a minister in the Church. The university is a free institution with a program of its own. Many of the graduates become teachers, journalists, or researchers, and then there are those who seek ordination.

The evening reception also served as a last-minute rehearsal for the big event. The Diocese lawyer was present to stress the importance of the holy oath of office we were about to take prior to the ordination service. Our lawyer was somewhat controversial, liked by some, very much disliked by others. We all agreed that he was very intelligent and skillful – fearful character traits if he happened to be an adversary. Church law was part of our study program. I had an affinity for the subject, and I liked our master too. Suddenly we all became quite serious. Our lawyer explained the oath we had to take that morning. The combination of his convincing voice and nonchalant attitude, a result of his familiarity with the subject, succeeded in capturing our attention completely.

"I can't do it," one of the candidates said, "This is getting too serious. My 'yes' is 'yes' and 'no' is 'no,' but I can't swear on the Bible to obey the Church for the rest of my life." The tension was rising. Was there to be an argument before the festivities? For the hesitant candidates, there was an alternative: one may give a solemn declaration instead of swearing on the Bible. That satisfied the scared candidate, but it created a stir that made us reexamine our situation and the significance of the step we were about to take.

At that moment I did not feel any need to rebel. I was prepared for this step, and by taking an oath on the Bible I was placing more emphasis on the Scripture than on the Church, that was, after all, the object of our oath. Nevertheless, I regarded the promise and oath to be a lifetime commitment, never to be broken.

In the lead-up to this momentous event, the ultimate joy and satisfaction was taken from me when my father – blessed be his memory – passed away suddenly, six months before my ordination. He had followed my studies intensively and was looking forward to my ordination. The rest of my immediate family attended the festivities. We gathered at the hotel in central Borga – my wife, mother, sister, and two brothers with their spouses, and my mother-in-law. Our baby girl Linda, who was a year and a half at the time, was at home with a babysitter. This was the second ordination in our family. Two years earlier we had witnessed my brother's ordination in Sweden. Birger had studied theology at the University of Uppsala and was ordained to the ministry in the Church of Sweden in Lulea in 1976. Now he had the privilege of being one of the assistants to the Bishop who officiated at my ordination ceremony. What could be more satisfying and meaningful than two brothers joining the priesthood.

My mother was not, by nature, an outspoken person, and at this time, she was particularly introverted since she was still very much in pain after losing her husband of nearly forty years. Although she did not express her feelings in words, I knew she was very happy for me and the family. Since I was the youngest in my family, my mother was anxious for me to receive an education and start an independent life, a life dedicated to God. The day of my ordination was therefore a victory for her faith and for her struggle.

She could now relax; her youngest child now held a respected profession and position.

My mother never said it, but in her own way, she conveyed a special message to me. It was reflected in the greeting she wrote on a gift she gave me, a small painting of my childhood home. Like Hanna in the Temple she wanted to offer her son to the service of the Almighty. Now two of her sons had become ministers in the Church. The greeting on the back of the painting was from Psalm 84:

> How lovely are thy dwelling places, O Lord of hosts. My soul longs, indeed, it faints for the courts of the Lord, my heart and my flesh cry out for the living God. Even the sparrow has found a home and a swallow a nest for herself, where she may lay her young. Thy altars, O Lord of hosts my King and my God. Happy are they who dwell in thy house; they are ever praising thee (Sela). Happy is the man whose strength is in thee in whose heart are thy highways, who passing through the valley of Bakha, turn into a waterspring; moreover the early rains cover it with blessings. They go from strength to strength, every one of them appears before God in Zion.

The Dome was packed. The candidates lined up in the sacristy, the room behind the altar for the ministers. We were dressed in the obligatory black caftan with its white collar. The caftan was tailor-made, very high quality and expensive, for it had to last for a long time. This knee-length black robe is the festive garment of a minister, worn to weddings, funerals and other occasions, and is comparable to a dress suit. The everyday clothing for a minister is a standard suit and black shirt with a white collar. But today was definitely a festive occasion and nothing but the best would do. The assistants walked behind us, and finally, the Bishop. When we entered the church, the organist and the trumpeter filled the old archways with magnificent chorales. An overwhelming feeling encompassed my whole being. We were displaced in time – medieval or modern, ancient or biblical – it did not matter. Everything was concentrated in this moment, the focal point of all of history. And now, my young life was connected with a history that was much more important than my own.

When the procession reached the front of the church we positioned ourselves in a semi-circle in front of the altar rail, ready to kneel for the blessing later during the service, after we had been dressed in our liturgical vestments. As with every other service in the Church, our ordination began in the name of the Triune God, announced by the officiating Bishop. All the candidates expressed their faith according to the creed of the Church. This creed talks about the Father, Son and Holy Spirit. Followed by our declarations of willingness to serve the Church and fight heresy, we were clothed in the clerical robes, the visible sign of being an ordained minister. These vestments were to be worn only when we would officiate at a church service. Among the assistants at our ceremony were personal friends of the candidates; others were invited because they were to become colleagues in the congregations where the candidates were assigned their first positions. I was privileged to have my own brother present. He was now clothing me with my clerical insignia. This was an important moment in my life. We were joined in double brotherhood with the same life mission – to serve God.

My ordination was a happy and satisfying occasion. This was how I understood Mother Linnea's message, written on the back of her gift to me for my ordination. "…For a day in thy courts is better than a thousand. I had rather be at the threshold in the house of my God, than dwell in the tents of wickedness."

The service was over. Now it was time for real life to begin. We headed to our new positions, assigned by the Bishop. I had made it clear that I preferred to be located in the west coast of the country. It seemed that the Bishop agreed, for my first congregation was in Vasa, where I was to serve as the junior minister with four senior colleagues.

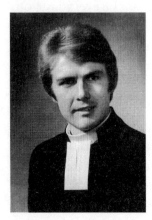

Newly ordained Minister Ole Brunell

THREE

In Search of Greener Pastures

THE CONGREGATION in Vasa treated me well, as did my colleagues. It was certainly a good place to practice, and I quickly learned the routine of the job. I was young and energetic, and I took my work seriously.

After a few years, during which time our second daughter, Sara, was born, I had gained enough experience to seek new horizons. My next challenge took me to the picturesque seaside town of Kristinestad, with fishing villages and farms. I was to be sole minister of this smaller congregation. This meant significantly more responsibility and also management of administrative tasks. I looked forward to working with "my own" church council and soon I learned that administering and organizing were my favorite duties, along with preaching, of course.

My congregation members were down-to-earth folk – "What you see is what you get." We lived in a beautiful, mansion-style, old vicarage. The new church was opposite our home. The old church had been destroyed in a fire a few years earlier, just before Christmas, an event that still haunted many of its members. The tall belltower was saved from the fire – a remnant of a bygone era – and still stood proudly on the church hill. The tower was still used as a landmark for sailors and fishermen when entering the port. Every Saturday at six in the evening, the bellringer announced the arrival of the day of rest, Sunday, by ringing a beautiful sequence of three bells. These bells played the same tune as the three bells in my hometown church. No wonder I felt at home in this little parish.

The age profile in the parish was quite old. There were more deaths per year than births. Most weeks we heard the same church bells announcing the departure of a dear soul. Family and friends of the departed would gather by the church to listen to the ringing when the "soul swung its way up to God," although the actual funeral was usually held a week after the death. Sharing both joyful and sorrowful moments with the parishioners can be a daunting task for a minister. It is also the time when parish members put their minister to the test. He has to provide his congregation with support, make visits to the hospital, to private homes, listen to their stories, understand, and sympathize. But during Sunday morning church service, it is the congregation's turn to listen. This is when the minister delivers his captivating, enthusiastic, and educational sermon of the week. Parish members can tolerate a lot, but they draw the line at dull sermons. I accepted these unspoken rules wholeheartedly. A minister must be at the service of his parishioners.

The people of Kristinestad accepted us warmly. When the news came that my wife had delivered twin girls, the congregation felt as if we had come to change the birthrate. Suddenly the parish began to grow. The birthrate had risen. Our youngest daughters, Karolin and Josefin, came into the world on their mother's birthday in May 1982. Only one month before, Runa had been skiing on the ice covering the Baltic Sea, as part of her regular exercise schedule. During a routine ultrasound check-up after the skiing trip, the doctor could see only one baby. The two were playing hide and seek. To our great joy Karolin and Josefin appeared healthy and beautiful, as had their older sisters, Linda and Sara before them. The midwife, herself childless, asked in all seriousness if she could adopt one of the twins. So identical were the two newborns that we kept one baby's thumbnail always painted red until they were old enough to tell us who was who.

* * *

I have always enjoyed new and demanding challenges. Little did I know that the visit my wife and I paid to her sister in Australia in 1983 would be a catalyst for a new and life-changing adventure. We totally fell in love with the vast and beautiful country. Having only traveled in Scandinavian countries, this was the first time we had enjoyed a warm climate. During our trip, we visited the Finnish Lutheran Church in Brisbane. The minister was completing a five-year term that was finishing shortly. I didn't feel excited, but without any doubt, from that moment I had my mind set on filling the vacancy. My wife supported me strongly, although there were many arguments against moving to Brisbane. The house provided for the minister was well below the standard of our home in Finland. And the language! Until now I had worked basically in Swedish. Suddenly I would have to preach in Finnish and English. We would have to uproot the children – how would they be affected? The question was, should we let the thought grow and develop or should we let it go?

We could not let it go. The fascination grew stronger and when the job became available in 1985, I applied. I had to compete with several other candidates, and was interviewed and tested, but was finally found suitable for the challenging job of taking care of the Scandinavian community in the furthest possible location from my homeland. Besides the language, the job itself did not differ greatly from my existing position, but every other aspect presented huge challenges. So we moved across the globe with a young family, not knowing then that it was a practice run for the life-changing thrill sixteen years later when we would make *aliyah* to Israel.

Our parishioners in Kristinestad, who had welcomed us so warmly, were sad to see us leave, but I was looking to the future and had no time for nostalgia. What saddened me, though, was the prospect of leaving my aging mother. It was bad enough when we lived but a three-hour drive away; now we were moving to the other side of the globe. As much as she loved her children and grandchildren, she had also learned the hard lesson of letting go at the right moment, and she accepted it.

On a cold, snowy April morning in 1985 we left our hometown and set off for Australia. A new adventure had begun.

Life is full of departures and arrivals, farewells and welcomes. We were only recovering from our sad departure from Finland when a new, happy welcome awaited us in Brisbane. A reunion with Runa's sister Gunlis, her husband Gunnar, and their family was followed by a welcome party at Bunya Street Finnish Chapel, organized by our new parish. The chairman of the congregation was a sugarcane farmer called Paavo, or Bob, as he was called in English. Ever since he had left his homeland thirty years earlier, in his youth, he had continued to speak the old Finnish language. His speech sounded strange and rough, yet direct.

"This is a tough place, a small congregation with limited resources, but we appreciate that you have come and we will do our best to ensure that you and your family will be happy here," Paavo said.

This attitude was quite typical of the people and the congregation, which consisted of laborers, farmers, and miners, only a few below the age of fifty. The congregation donated generously and expected a reasonable return. I, in turn, was determined to do the best job I could, not knowing exactly what they had in mind other than pastoral services.

We began our new life in Brisbane with some bumps along the way; it was challenging to have to adjust to such an unfamiliar and foreign environment. For our family, Australia was a whole new world. The older girls started school immediately. Linda, as the oldest, took on the responsibility of setting the pace for the others. With her head held high, she went to school from the first day without knowing one word of English. Sara, who was only five, went with her and started first grade. Three days in a row, Sara went to school with tears running down her cheeks. She was obviously unhappy. I couldn't blame her. She was unable to express herself and did not understand a word that was being spoken to her. After three days, she suddenly stopped crying and explained that God helped her when she prayed. In hindsight, starting school this way must have been quite traumatic, but fortunately our daughters managed and did well. Karolin and Josefin had a softer landing in this new environment. They still had time for lots of innocent mischief before they needed to think about the serious business of school. It did not take long before our daughters communicated in their new language, and until today they speak English to each other and to us, even though we answer in Swedish.

On the same street as the Lutheran church was a Catholic chapel and a synagogue. If I happened to mention in conversation that I was Lutheran, I was usually asked: "What is that?" Most Australians are either Catholic or Anglican. My job was similar to my previous one in Finland, but the challenge, I soon understood, was to arrange events that provided some financial relief to the members of my congregation. The emphasis on fundraising was new to me. In Finland all Lutheran congregations are supported by the state with tax revenues, but this was certainly not Finland. The fundraising methods were as diverse and varied as creativity would allow. In addition to charging a membership fee, we organized everything from lotteries and bazaars to picnics and food festivals. Lotteries were a contentious issue. The Australian Lutheran Church was unfamiliar with this method of fundraising, and certainly did not approve – what are these Finns thinking of! Once we had a big catch for the prize in a lottery. The famous golfer Greg Norman had a Finnish grandmother who regularly attended our church services and lived only a block away. She asked her grandson, the "Great White Shark," as he is famously known, for a golf glove to be used as first prize in our fundraising lottery. Needless to say, our parish fund enjoyed a nice boost.

I did not mind working as a fundraiser, but I certainly felt that a minister had other priorities to think about. So we began organizing services in Swedish. There is a large Scandinavian community in Brisbane that did not have any regular Church services in Swedish. With Swedish as my mother tongue, I was more than happy to initiate this cooperative service. For my Finnish parish it meant assistance with the Church fund, so Paavo and the rest of the Church council were quick to approve the idea. This co-existence proved to be mutually beneficial and harmonious, and to this day, the Finnish minister still provides services in Swedish.

Years went by and the work continued and developed. I had a good working relationship with my colleagues in the Australian Lutheran Church, although I mostly worked alone, except for the company of my wife, of course, who was the organist in the church. That was the nature of the job. The closest Finnish minister partner was approximately 800 km away in Sydney. We met regularly, which, under these circumstances, meant once or twice a year. The annual summer camp was a real treat for the entire family. Since the different congregations organized these camps we managed to visit all the major cities of Australia. Driving home from one such camp, through the desert from Adelaide to Brisbane in a heat wave without air-conditioning, is an experience none of us will easily forget.

Australia was a truly enjoyable adventure. Was there anything at all in our Australian experience that initiated my religious questioning? What possibly could have been the reason for my doubt in so many of the Church's basic teachings? I cannot point my finger at any specific moment or event. Was the questioning within me latent, all the time accompanying my soul, just waiting for the right time to emerge? Runa and I read the Bible together, as we knew it then, with the two parts. If the Tanach was the basis, why was the so-called New Testament so different?

Looking back, I remember the seeds of my doubts. It was connected to the Church practice of baptism. In a way baptism was my favorite event. A baby had been born, the family was united, a good reason to celebrate. The old practice is to have the baptism a week after the birth. Today the time frame is more negotiable and can stretch up to a month. Usually, I held a meeting with the family to explain the meaning of this sacrament. We discussed which hymns to sing, who would be the Godparents and other issues related to the family-church event. Should the baptism take place at home or in the church? Both practices were accepted. I explained to the parents how this sacrament is important because it makes the child a member of the Holy Church, which is the New Israel. When I made the sign of the cross on the forehead and on the breast of the child, this was a sign that the one who was crucified had redeemed him from all his sins. The parents, who might have forgotten what they themselves learned in their confirmation class, had their memory refreshed of the responsibility of raising their child in the faith of the Church. As I heard myself speak to the new parents, I suddenly realized that the teachings of the Church were inconsistent with the words of the Bible. Why? Warning bells started to ring.

The Vicarage provided by the seaside parish in Kristinestad

F O U R

Seeds of Doubt

ONE NIGHT, I woke up in a sweat after a nightmare. In the dream that tormented me, I was trapped in my pulpit during a sermon and about to suffocate to death, as if somebody had forced a plastic bag over my head. It felt so real. I was going to die. This is precisely what would have happened to me spiritually had I not acted upon these internal warnings. Trying to ignore the signals would have been the same as ignoring traffic lights. You must obey them, or risk injury or death.

These thoughts were developing during the latter period of our stay in Australia, in the late 1980s. After the nightmare, I had tremendous difficulty speaking from the pulpit, especially in one of the churches we used for our Sunday services. This particular building was quite old for a new country like Australia, and the pulpit was the "barrel style," where the priest steps up along high stairs with only his head protruding above the edge of the podium. Inside the "barrel" there was a small platform to stand on. My predecessor was obviously quite short, so he had constructed an aid, which made him, and also me, stand a few inches taller. It was of some help. Once up there in the podium, I wanted to see the people beneath me. But getting into that barrel became impossible for me. I decided to deliver my sermon from the floor. There I felt closer to the people, as if I could whisper a secret in their ears, a secret that could not be uttered from the pulpit. From high up in the pulpit, a minister speaks with a kind of formal authority. He is not an individual with his own subjective opinions. His message is sealed with the stamp of the institution. He may even be on fire with that message and captivate his audience with those words, as long as he believes them.

I was on fire. I used to love setting other people on fire until there was no more fuel to burn. I asked myself, how come there is not enough fuel? If this is the eternal truth, there has to be enough. I knew there was plenty of wood for the fire in the Scriptures, but all the conflicts I was beginning to see functioned like buckets of water on a bonfire. They gave smoke and steam but the glow was dying.

Physically coming down to the same level as the congregation gave me a new perspective on my role. As I came closer to the people I could be more personally involved. I felt less obligated by the official dogmas of the Church, and was more attracted to revealing the secrets I was uncovering in the Tanach. At the same time I realized that I had not actually discovered something new or unique. How could it be? I was simply reading the plain text of the Tanach, the same text that is, after all, available to anybody who wishes to access it. My focus was shifting, and my loyalties changing.

It is often much easier to explain what happened than why it all happened. This is certainly true when talking about the different chapters of my life, from the ministry of the Church to my conversion to Judaism. The huge changes in my life were the equivalent of moving from the position of teacher to that of a student, once again. Why would anybody put himself in that position?

Religion was not a "hobby" for me – it was my profession and my whole life. I was not a private person who could separate my faith from my public life. It might be possible to play the role of the good minister, even if the minister's personal beliefs differ from the teachings of the Church. For me, however, this was not a solution. My faith was my livelihood. If I couldn't believe it, I couldn't teach it. When I started to doubt the basic teachings of the Church, and the validity of certain sacraments, I gradually lost my ability to perform. Slowly but surely it became more and more difficult for me to perform the sacraments of baptism and communion and to deliver a sermon.

What amazes me is the fact that the cards were on the table, all the time, yet I never saw them. I learned to critically question the text of the Bible, but did not raise an eyebrow over the fact that this great institution officially taught about a Triune God that was nowhere to be found in the Holy Book. Every ceremony and service in the Church starts and finishes in the name of the Triune God. That is, "the name of the Father, Son and Holy Spirit." The name itself is not mentioned, but this formula is always repeated. So too, the Aaronic benediction was instituted as the formula used by Christian ministers as blessings at every wedding, baptism or funeral service. The original formula for this blessing is found in the Tanach in Numbers 6, when God tells Moshe to tell Aaron how to bless the children of Israel.

"The Lord bless thee and keep thee;
The Lord make his face shine upon thee, and be gracious onto
    thee;
The Lord lift up His countenance to thee and give thee peace."

The Church adopted this formula for conveying the divine blessing to its people, but not without making some changes, of course. The original text is used in full, but the formula for the Triune God is added at the end. By examining the original context of this formula, we learn that the *Cohanim*, the Jewish priests, by using this blessing, put the name of Hashem on the Israelites. "And they shall put My name upon the children of Israel and I will bless them" (Numbers 6:27). The Church is not blessing its people in the name of only one God but in the name of the Triune God – God the Father, God the Son and God the Holy Spirit.

I remember as a child, every spring I would observe migrating birds in our garden. We were always waiting for them; when they came it was a sign of spring, and that meant the summer was near. I always wondered where these birds really lived, since they came to us only for a short visit. They built their nests, as if in a hurry, knowing that the Finnish summer is very short. One day soon after, we would see the young birds flying out of their nests. The summer had passed its peak, and we saw flocks of swallows, starlings and wagtails on their way south. Imagine, these birds are born in the Scandinavian summer, and when the fall approaches, they know it is time to leave, and they fly away, led only by instinct. They were born in Finland, and have never been to their new destination, yet these birds still know that they belong somewhere else, and they leave for a warmer place.

The same applies to me. I feel as if I had just paid a short visit to the country of my birth and made a brief incursion into a strange religion called Christianity. I had a desire to pursue the truth, which I had begun to see, a desire to come closer to God's Land and His chosen people. I had an urge to leave the institution that made me feel as if I were a betrayer. That's not to say that I blame the average Christian churchgoer. Everybody needs religiosity in his or her life. The customs and traditions of Christianity make life seem beautiful throughout all the various life cycle events, and even in death, and the fellowship is uplifting, healing, and comforting.

Yet in the midst of all these strong traditions, where is the search for truth? Where is the drive for consistency in the theological manuscript among the leaders? The ministers and the Bishops possess the knowledge and the history, they study the Tanach and they are exposed to the inconsistencies spelled out in the text.

After more than a decade outside the Christian Church, with half of that time spent living in Israel as a Jew, I have had the opportunity to reflect on the issues that became the obstacles to my continuing with the Church. It became crystal clear to me that the Church is not based on truth found in the Holy Book. The decision of one family might not have much impact in the world; the Christian Church has, after all, thrived for 2,000 years. Still, I maintain that the evidence I have against the Church, as a true institution, is very strong. The big surprise is *where* most of this evidence is to be found: in Christianity's own writings, the so-called New Testament. My faith is probably the greatest asset God gave me. Therefore I believed in what I had discovered, and I realized that these discoveries were to have consequences. Yet it was not enough to believe, I also had to act.

After weighing all the options there was one thing that tipped the scale in favor of my leaving the Church – inner conviction or instinct. I felt a strong drive that once and for all pushed me out of the large institution that is Christianity.

The Tanach hints at an instinct in animals that drove them to enter the Ark of Noah. In *Parashat* Noah (Genesis 7:1–10), we are told how Noah was commanded to enter the Ark with his family because the Flood was about to begin. To save not only human life, but also the lives of all living things, he had to bring into the ark one pair of each animal according to their species. "Of the clean (kosher) animal, of the animal that is not clean, of the birds, and of each thing that creeps upon the ground, two by two they came to Noah into the Ark, male and female, as God had commanded Noah" (Genesis 7:8–9). The great commentator Ramban comments that God caused one pair of each species to instinctively find refuge in the Ark.

Without delving into an in-depth analysis of the history of the Church, there are plain and simple examples of how a small Jewish sect, hoping for the Moshiach in their struggle against the Romans, turned out to be useful to the Romans. Once taken over by pagans during the third and fourth century CE, the Church was turned into a political institution manipulated and dictated by Rome. This tool in itself was used to enhance the power of the state. So powerful was the structure of this newly instituted "tool" that it survived its master, the Roman Empire, and became the new political power player seated in Rome. This institution calls itself the New Israel. The Pope sees himself as the successor to Apostle Peter, who, according to the tradition, was given the keys to heaven and hell, life and death. The one who has the keys holds the power, therefore the Church has had the authority to keep its followers with statements such as "outside the Church – no salvation." Considering their immense power, it is a pity that the Catholic Church cannot open the Vatican Archive to researchers. It is believed to hold answers to many mysteries and controversial decisions during the long history of this institution, from its early days until the tragic stand by the Church during the Holocaust in our time.

Over the centuries, hundreds of different denominations have evolved from the institution. One of them is the Lutheran Church formed during the late 1500s by Martin Luther, originally a Catholic monk.

Christianity is not a monotheistic religion, although it is generally regarded as such. How could it be monotheistic when there is a choice between praying to God the Father, or to Jesus Christ, or to a third alternative, the Holy Spirit? Does this constitute idol worship? It obviously is not in the strictest sense of the word, since Christians don't believe that god takes the form of a statue, but believing that a human being is god is also idol worship. This is the opinion of both Ramban and Rabbi Kook. Bowing in front of the crucifix when approaching the altar, in order to receive the bread and wine in the Holy Communion, indicates reverence for this idol. Christians are taught that the visible insignia of this sacrament, the bread and wine, are the body and blood of Jesus. Ask any Christian believer, and he will tell you the importance of the Trinity, that God is three. If a Christian betrays any hesitation in the belief that God is three, it is regarded as a lack of faith in the divinity of Jesus. Not embracing the "truth" of Jesus's divinity is the most heretical thought and cannot be accepted. The "apostolic confession of faith," confessed publicly in every Sunday church service clearly states: "I believe in God, the Father Almighty Creator of heaven and earth…I believe in Jesus Christ His only begotten Son, born of virgin Mary, conceived by the Holy Spirit…I believe in the Holy Spirit….” Not a single statement that God is One. The Church declares its faith in three gods, but the founder of the faith expresses his faith in ONE GOD, demonstrating how the Church is not even true to the beliefs of its own founder. Once asked what is the most important confession, he simply answered as any Jew would: “*Shema Yisrael*…Hear O Israel, The Lord our God the Lord is one” (Mark 12:28). But not so his followers.

The Church is not the New Israel, as it claims. Declaring a new covenant, it renders the original covenant null and void. There is a claim in the Christian New Testament that: “By speaking of a new covenant, God has made the first one old, and anything that becomes old and worn out will soon disappear” (Book of Hebrews 8:13). In theological terms this is called “replacement theology.” So where is the real Israel? Strictly speaking it should not exist. Christian scholars admitted in 1948, when the State of Israel was born, that this fact was “a very problematic theological dilemma.” As far as I know the “Old” is still alive and well, despite so many enemies and struggles.

It is generally accepted that the universal laws in the Tanach given to all mankind are the seven Noahide laws as explained in Genesis. These laws were imparted to all of humanity after the Flood some 700 years before the Torah was given to the Jews. After the Flood, God promises Noah that He will never again destroy all earthly life with a natural catastrophe. The sign for this covenant was the rainbow in the sky. Corresponding to the seven laws there are seven colors in the rainbow.

A debate in the Book of Acts in the New Testament argues whether or not to impose all the Mosaic Law on the believers of the new faith. The decision taken by the apostles is not to impose all the Jewish laws upon the people, but strictly limit these to the seven Noahide laws as binding for everyone. This is very clear and straightforward, at least so it seems. Still there is confusion in the Lutheran Church, and other denominations as well, as to how to teach this. For example, there is no clear teaching about the prohibition of eating blood, a very clear prohibition in both the Old and New Testaments. In Finland, where much of the population belongs to the Lutheran Church, which still has influence on the daily life of the people, there is no protest when the hot meal served to children in state schools regularly consists of blood patties with lingonberry jam. How could the eating of blood be forbidden when in every communion service the priest encourages the congregation to partake in the holy communion and drink the blood of Jesus?

A non-Jew can, but does not have to, convert to Judaism. Converts are accepted, but Judaism is definitely not a missionary religion. In the Messianic era Judaism will no longer accept converts, probably for the same reason that it is too late to take a test after you have seen the results. What are important are the seven Noahide laws as found in Genesis 9. These form the basis for the conduct of human life, both on a private and social level. In Encyclopedia Britannica we find one of the most accurate descriptions of the seven Noahide laws: "…a Jewish Talmudic designation for seven biblical laws given to Adam and to Noah before the revelation to Moses on Mt. Sinai and consequently binding on all mankind" (The New Encyclopedia Britannica: Micropedia, 15th ed., vol. 8, p. 737).

1. We are created in God's image, respect Him, and do not worship an idol. 2. Be careful with your words, do not curse in the name of God. 3. Life is a gift, respect it, do not murder. 4. Do not commit adultery. Value family and marriage as the base of society. 5. Respect the property of others, therefore do not steal. 6. Every creature has a soul, literally, "do not eat a limb torn from a living animal." Show therefore kindness to all creatures. 7. Establish a court system and pursue justice.

"How generally accepted the Seven Noahide laws are can be seen in the Joint Resolution by the Senate and the House of Representatives of the USA resolved on March 26, 1991. The statement designates a special Education Day whereby Congress recognizes the historical tradition of the ethical values and principles that have been the bedrock of society from the dawn of civilization, when they were known as the Seven Noahide Laws" (*Law and the Noahides*, Prof. Nahum Rakover, p. 125).

These rules are general guidelines given by God to all mankind before the time of any institutional religions. Later, during history, the same God gave more specific laws in the Holy Torah to the Jewish people. For a non-Jew, these seven laws are binding. Throughout the world we already see a growing number of people from Christian Churches leaving their denominations to form Noahide congregations. I believe this will be a fast growing movement in the future. We see people leaving their false religions and returning to the basic truth of the Tanach as expressed in these seven laws. The Church as a political institution will be dismantled together with its theological structure and replaced with communities of people who believe in One God. Fellowships of believers will turn away from prayer to various gods, concentrating their renewed spiritual communication to God – the Only One.

God gave the Holy Torah to Moses and subsequently to all the Jews. This happened at a certain place and time in history, and was witnessed by all of *Am Yisrael*. When was the New Testament given? And to whom was it directed? The authors of the New Testament blatantly place themselves above the Torah in their writings, ignoring the warning in the Torah that says: "You shall not add to the word that I command you, nor shall you subtract from it, to observe the commandments of Hashem, your God, that I command you" (Deuteronomy 4:1–2). So how did the authors of the New Testament handle this issue? They ignored the existing warning and added one of their own to the end of the last book in the New Testament. In the Book of Revelation the apostle John says: "I warn everyone who hears the words of prophecy of this book: if anyone adds anything to them, God will add to him the plagues described in this book. And if anyone takes words away from this book of prophecy, God will take away from his share in the tree of life and in the holy city, which are described in this book."

The Church has transformed the words of man into the words of God by proclaiming the New Testament to be a Holy Book. The original God-given Torah has been replaced by a sample of letters written by man. The New Testament, written by man, annuls the Torah given by God, although it preserves some of its teachings, believing them to be useful. Speaking of the Torah, the Book of Hebrews in the Christian New Testament says: "The old rule, then, is set aside, because it was weak and useless. For the Law of Moses could not make anything perfect. And now a better hope has been provided through which we come near to God" (Book of Hebrews 7:18–19).

These are serious accusations levelled against Judaism by the Christian Holy Book. For this reason, the underlying feeling of Christians towards Jews is one of superiority, because, as stated in their New Testament, they have something better than the "old law" which is "weak and useless and will disappear" (Book of Hebrews). At the same time, this attitude is tainted with jealousy because the Jews have Abraham, Moses, David, and all the rest. The Christians believe that one day the Jews will accept Jesus, and great blessings will await them. Undoubtedly there are also groups of Christians who sincerely support and bless Israel out of the pure faith that their God is the God of Israel.

In my reflections on the Christian Church and its beliefs, years after leaving the fold, I continue to be amazed at the amount of clear evidence against the validity of the main issues in Christianity, some of which I have commented on above.

There is one analogy I would like to make, which sums up the complexity and gravity of both the accusations and the case.

Let's call it the "Moses-complex," dating back to the time of the Exodus when the Israelite nation prepared itself to receive the Torah. Moses, as the prophetic leader of the Nation, would talk to God on behalf of the people, and at the same time, talk to the people on behalf of God. The nation learned to live with a mediator, a physical being, who represented them before God, and who also represented God to them. When they were to receive the Torah, Moses went up the mountain for forty days. This was a long time for them to wait. The people became impatient. They believed Moses had died and they desperately needed something to worship. God was too holy and too distant to approach directly. Remembering the statue gods in Egypt, they decided to make a god for themselves, and convinced Aaron to make a golden calf.

We all know the result. The sounds of the festival, of people celebrating and dancing around the man-made god, rose up the mountain. Moses was on his way down. He was furious. How could he intervene this time? God punished the people who had turned to idol worship. The message was clear: worship no idol! But they still had Moses. He continued to teach and guide them and pray for them until his time was complete and Joshua took over. After entering the Promised Land the nation still had leaders and prophets with authority. The Judges, the Kings and Prophets – they all served the purpose of summoning the soul of the nation. After Malakhi, the last of the prophets, who lived about 400 years Before the Common Era (BCE), we no longer had prophesy. The nation's longing for the Moshiach grew stronger; they desperately needed a savior to redeem them from the oppressive powers, the Greeks and the Romans in turn. By the end of the Second Temple period, the people had seen nothing close to the authority or spiritual leadership of Moses for centuries.

It was against this background and atmosphere that Jesus came along.

He did not turn out to be the Moshiach they had long been waiting for, but his followers made him a mediator between man and God. The apostles started to teach that you can approach God only through this man from Nazareth. After his death his followers declared that since he did not fulfill the expectations of Moshiach during his lifetime, he will come again and complete the job at a later date. Soon the main focus of these events shifted from the Jewish people to the gentiles. During coming decades and centuries, Jesus's status changed from that of a mediator to one of a god to be worshipped, the exclusive savior without whom one is doomed to hell. A few centuries into the common era, the Church, which by then was dominated by non-Jews, established a decree stating that Jesus was god and had to be worshipped equally to the Father in heaven. The symbol for this god is the crucifix – to be found in every church. Christians bow before the crucifix to show respect – some even kiss it. Whenever Christians pray, the prayer must be in the name of Jesus.

I call this phenomenon the "Moses-complex." What happened during a forty-day period in the desert can be seen here as a development over a few centuries. A people who longed for Moses ended up with a golden calf. The second time around, the people longed for a Savior and ended up with a god called Jesus.

Jesus became to the Christian world what the golden calf was to the Israelites during Moses's absence. This god was convenient. He was always there, visible and tangible. He was approachable. He was not demanding; on the contrary, he always forgave and understood. His followers became dependent on him because the only way to survive and to be purged of sin was through his intervention. Therefore it became difficult to let go of this man-made god.

There is a similarity between the golden calf cult and the worshipping of Jesus in Christianity. The "Moses-complex" created this phenomenon and gave the gentile world a substitute for the God they never knew.

When the news disseminates from Jerusalem, hopefully in our time, that the Jews are crowning Moshiach as King of Israel, this will not be the kind of news the Christians are anticipating. The breaking news of this historical event will pave the way for all nations to believe in the One and Only God of Israel.

How can I make such bold statements against Christianity? Why is this institution still influential if it is based on error? People have a great inner need for spirituality and religiosity. Whoever tends to this basic human need will acquire followers. This can be said for the Christian Church. Christianity is an easy religion and the holidays are beautiful. Think about Christmas and all the family gatherings, decorations, presents, or the glory of an early morning Easter service. Christianity also has the "license" to execute all the rites of passage during the cycle of life, beginning with baptism after a birth, confirmation upon entering adulthood, marriage, and finally the burial ceremony. Rituals celebrating rites of passage are found in all cultures and religions. As long as Christianity can maintain a broad contact with mainstream citizens through these rituals and ceremonies, it will remain intact. Although some of the rites touch existential questions, such as life and death, or the purpose of life, the big theological issues can always be avoided. It is one thing to be a good adviser and comforter, as most ministers are in these situations, and quite another to question the consistency and truth of significant theological issues, such as monotheism, Moshiach and the Word of God.

To me, the evidence against the trustworthiness of Christianity became a burden too heavy to bear. I could no longer harbor the responsibility of sharing in that faith. Since I could not change the teaching or influence the believers, the only option left to me was to step out of that framework, abandon the lifestyle and environment. The irony is that the strongest evidence against Christianity is its own holy book, the New Testament. In Christianity I could still find enough traces of truth that led me back to its origins. This search took me to Judaism, where the truth and vigor of the old theology drew me like iron filings to a magnet. I was not only pushed out of the Church by its falsehoods, but also pulled towards Judaism by its fascinating authenticity.

One basic and very important teaching within the Church is the divine birth of Jesus, a person whom the Christians claim to be the Moshiach (Messiah). On the first page of the Christian New Testament, two claims are made simultaneously, but they don't gel. Matthew, the disciple of Jesus and writer of the first book of the Christian Holy Book, explains how Joseph, the husband-to-be of Mary who gave birth to Jesus, is of the line of David. This supports the idea that Jesus could be the Moshiach, since the Christians agree with the Jews that the Moshiach has to be of the line of David. Matthew's next statement, however, is that Joseph is not the father of Jesus. Rather, his paternal origin is divine and he is actually conceived by the Holy Spirit; that is, by God himself. What further complicates the story is that even Joseph was taken by surprise by Mary's pregnancy. She is reported to have been pregnant before they were married under the chuppah. An angel informs Joseph that the pregnancy is of divine origin and encourages him to still take her as his wife.

This is like trying to place three pieces in a two-piece puzzle. Whatever way you look at the problem you have one piece left over. Since when has a two-piece puzzle been complicated anyway? Is Jesus the Son of Joseph or is he the Son of God? He cannot be both. The third piece in this puzzle is the claim that he is the Moshiach. If Jesus is the Son of God born of Virgin Mary, as the Church claims, then he is not of the line of David, since Joseph was not his father, and consequently he cannot be the Moshiach. If, again, he is born with Joseph as his father and of Davidic lineage, he is not of divine origin, in opposition to the most vital Church dogma that Jesus is God. This simple equation is open for everybody to see on the first page of the New Testament, but nobody questions it.

Why is it forbidden to question the teaching? Because it is more important to uphold the institution! Loyalty must be directed towards the tradition of the Church rather than to the Bible. If there is a discrepancy between the Bible and the accepted teachings of the institution, one is obliged to follow the official teaching. Furthermore there are always explanations.

The more I opened my eyes to these questions, the more rebellious I started to feel toward the institution. And there are many more questions. It is not just a two-piece puzzle, but a puzzle of two thousand pieces.

What of Sunday, the day of rest? Is it found in the Tanach? No! So why is it so important in the eyes of the Church? Doesn't the Torah teach that Shabbat, the seventh day of the week, is the day sanctified by God for the purpose of Torah study, prayer, and rest – the day when God rested after His six days of creation? During the early centuries of Christian history, when the Church was institutionalized and politicized, Sunday, rather than Saturday, was designated as the Christian Sabbath, in order to differentiate between Christians and Jews. The Christians claim to celebrate Sunday because Jesus was said to have risen from the dead on the first day of the week. When the new religion became a state affair in the Roman Empire, it was also convenient to combine this day with the day the pagans worshipped the sun (sun-day). Another god has another day! Far-reaching decisions about the calendar and some important festivals were finalized in the Church council meetings in Nicaea in the year 325 of the Common Era (CE) and repeated in 381 CE. It was decided that the date of Easter, which was celebrated simultaneously with Passover, must be changed. The political majority decision was more authoritative than the Torah. It was also a deliberate step by the Church to separate itself from the Jews and create a new religion with its own calendar and festivals. They took a festival that was originally Jewish, Passover, and created a new one, Easter. This is a very familiar pattern in the formation of Christianity.

In more recent history, the European Union took a formal decision that Sunday must be regarded as the day of rest in the whole EU.

"The weekly day of rest must extend over at least twenty-four consecutive hours, and it must be Sunday." The law, instituted by the forerunner to the EU, the EC, on 1st August 1988, was updated by the European Union on 23rd February 2001.

"In principle, the law prohibits Sunday work. Workers whose religion does observe a day of rest on a day other than a Sunday may opt for Friday or Saturday, a footnote to the law explains.

During the first centuries CE, there was already another religion – the new Christianity, which had to fight for its existence. The fight was first directed against the Jews. In history this fight has repeated itself with varying intensity until its culmination during the Holocaust. The horror of the Holocaust was not a result of a direct battle between the Church and the Jews, but rather stemmed from the Church's philosophy. Their notion that the "New Israel" was to replace the real Israel gave nourishment to the thought of extinguishing the Jewish people. Martin Luther, the German priest who protested against the Catholic faith in 1500 CE, and in whose name a large Protestant Church was formed, inspired the Nazis through his writings. Martin Luther tried to win the Jews over to his side in his battle with the authorities. When he failed to gain support from the stubborn Jews, he turned against them and encouraged his followers to burn their synagogues. Martin Luther's pamphlet "About the Jews" is said to have had an influence on Hitler – may his name be blotted out. It is quite revealing, if not coincidental, that Kristallnacht, the first large-scale, German government-sponsored pogrom of the Second World War, took place on November 9, 1938, the eve of Martin Luther's birthday. He was born on November 10, 1483, in Eisleben, Germany, and died on February 17, 1546.

Another area of conflict is Christianity's adoption of Jewish symbols and practices. These symbols are familiar to Christians, as they are mentioned in the Tanach. They provide a feeling of confidence and security, of being on the right track, connected to history. But look a little deeper and we see that the content is different, or the meaning completely new, often to the extent that these new symbols negate the original purpose of the practice.

For example, there are biblical roots to the practice of baptism, but the different Christian denominations fight over its meaning and how it should be practiced. The mainstream Churches follow the tradition of baptizing infants, whereas some Protestant Churches baptize adults. What does this mean?

Every Jew knows that the symbol of the Covenant with Abraham is circumcision. This is carried out on the eighth day after the birth of a Jewish boy, according to the command given by God to our forefather. Another important ritual in Judaism is the *mikvah* (ritual bath). Here women immerse themselves after menstruation. This is an important part of the Jewish laws of family purity. During the time of the Temple, both men and women were obligated to immerse themselves in the *mikvah* before entering the Temple area. Today there are different traditions that dictate how often men go to the *mikvah*. Some go every week before Shabbat, most men only before the High Holidays, but the idea remains the same. The purpose of the *mikvah* is spiritual purification. Therefore, a person converting to Judaism must also immerse in the waters of the *mikvah* to cleanse himself of his old life, to become like a newborn with a pure soul.

The Church needed a ritual through which new members were grafted into this "New Israel." The result was a combination of circumcision and *mikvah*. The babies are carried to the ritual purification bath of baptism at the early age of one week to be made a member of the Church. The statement repeated at every baptism is the conviction that this ceremony makes the infant a member of the so-called "New Covenant" and an heir to the World to Come. This cleansing bath is needed even for infants, because according to Lutheran theology every person is born a sinner.

The Ten Commandments play an important role in Christian theology and education. Every confirmation class, in which Christian teenagers are introduced to the basic teachings of the Church, is confronted with the contents of the commandments and is tested on their knowledge of these pillars of biblical education. How many commandments did Moses receive at Mount Sinai? Ten. Yet, as a teacher I could not ask my confirmation class students to look up the commandments in the Tanach, although this is the original source. Instead we had to follow the textbook of the Church. Why? By the time Martin Luther was reforming the Church, and forming a Protestant denomination that would carry his name, the churches were full of statues and pictures. This was problematic, as the second commandment clearly forbade images. The solution was simple. Martin Luther excluded the prohibition of carved images and divided the last commandment into two in order to keep the total of ten. It was easier than removing the beautiful statues.

A similar attitude towards the word of God is unimaginable in Judaism. In the public Torah reading in the synagogue, even a mispronunciation of a single letter by the Torah reader is quickly corrected by the Gabbai. And an incorrectly written letter in a Torah scroll must be corrected before the Torah Scroll can be used again.

Again and again, the tragic fact repeats itself: Instead of conforming the teaching according to the Tanach, the Tanach is changed to fit the Church.

The ritual of communion, said to be instituted by Jesus during his Last Supper, with his disciples at the Passover Seder before his crucifixion, is celebrated regularly in the Christian Church service, on a weekly or monthly basis, depending on the local tradition. The visual contents of this ritual – bread and wine – symbolizing the body and blood of Jesus, offer forgiveness for sins and assure believers of a share in the World to Come. During the Middle Ages, uneducated people heard the priest announcing in Latin, "hoc est corpus meum…" – the beginning of the sentence that proclaims how the bread and wine turned into the body and blood of Jesus. The meaning of the words is "this is my body and this is my blood," but since the people did not understand the words, they simply heard them as "hocus-pocus filiokus…."

Slowly, one by one, these examples began to worry me. They acted as warning signals telling me that something was wrong, just as blinking red lights on the dashboard force you to stop driving. I felt guilty. As long as I was in the institution, I was misleading people. I was part of the plot falsifying the true word of God, as stated in His Torah. I was in the wrong camp.

Would it be possible to transform the Church? The thought crossed my mind for a second. What about fighting it? It would not be worth it. Step by step, painfully slowly, I started to realize that the fight I had to take upon myself was the battle to get out.

Like a fighter who sometimes has to use smoke bombs to protect himself, give himself time and room to maneuver, I also used similar tricks. For my own protection, and to satisfy my conscience by heading in the right direction, I started with small steps. This also indicated to the congregation that something was going on, without causing uproar or protest. My first "smoke bomb" was connected to the priestly blessing. Since I was very much disturbed with the added ending referring to the Triune God, I simply left it out and stopped as if I was quoting from the Book of Numbers.

My wife, the organist in the congregation, was well informed of this small, private plot against the Church, so she was quick to respond "Amen" with full volume on the organ right after the third sentence. The first time this happened it went almost unnoticed. People simply assumed that my wife was too quick and overwhelmed me with the ending. When this continued, however, it started to concern the congregation. The only explanation I ever gave for this change in liturgy was that I started to read the benediction from the Tanach instead of from the handbook – the minister's "*siddur*" for the service. This explanation satisfied some, but obviously it was not going to work for very long. I was turning to the Tanach instead of the Church's handbook. This was the source of the problem.

My time in Australia was running out. I came to Brisbane Finnish Lutheran Church with the intention of staying for five years. Technically I could have continued, and nobody would have been happier than my wife and daughters if we had stayed on. We all loved Australia. And to this day I know that we would have had a good, easy life in many respects if we had stayed Down Under. Still, it was impossible for me to meet all the challenges of leaving the Church while I was "away from home." If I had to leave, I had to at least confront the people back home, the Bishop, the community. Yet why couldn't I have gone back, finished what I had to do and returned to Queensland, the Australian Sunshine State? That could have spared us many sorrows and hardships. Wrong or not – who can tell? Who can fully understand the mysterious ways in which God works?

Upon our return to Finland, we would have to find a place to live, and a community in which to belong. I had to find a position for myself as if nothing were amiss. Suspecting that I would not stay with the Church for very long, I still applied for a minister's vacancy. There was an attractive position available in Tampere, one of the largest cities in Finland, and the congregation elected me.

There I was, fighting with my doubts about the Church, while committing to one more position, not knowing how soon everything would be over. This was a huge dilemma for me, but until I had arrived at a clear decision, I had to continue keeping up appearances. I couldn't announce a "possible" exit from the Church. I was either in or out, there was no middle ground.

During the farewell party with the congregation in Brisbane, my wife, who was always strong in her belief, said some very meaningful words that would come to have an even deeper meaning a few years later. She could not find any other reason for leaving Australia than to follow her husband. The words that came to her mind then were those of Ruth in the Tanach, when she said to her mother-in-law, "your God is my God and your people are my people, where you go I will go and where you die I will die." With tears in her eyes she accepted leaving Australia, her sister, and her family.

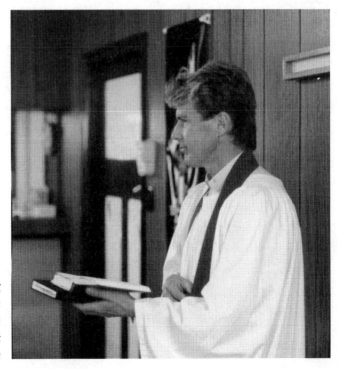

Ole Brunell conducting a Church service in the Finnish Lutheran Chapel on Bunya Street in Brisbane, Australia

The Brunell. Family in Australia surrounded by Queensland gum-trees

FIVE

Fighting the Tide

AFTER TWELVE YEARS as a minister in the Lutheran Church, including five years in Australia, we were now back in Finland, where I was serving as the head of a parish in central Finland. During the last years my confidence in the Church, or the institution, as I would rather call it, had gradually dropped to zero.

The drama that was about to unfold in public had already erupted in my mind months earlier. Somehow aware of the impossibility of my continuing as a minister in the Church, I still accepted the new position and uprooted my family from a settled life in Brisbane, Australia, to the Finnish city of Tampere.

As if this transition would not have been difficult enough for my family, who loved it "Down Under," we still had to face the fact that I was going to quit my job, the only livelihood I had ever known. Deep inside I knew that I could not continue in the Church, but for the time being I also knew I had to face the people on my home ground – including the Bishop, the church council, and of course our relatives. I could not quit from a distance.

The summer of 1990 was cool and quiet. The color of the horizon, however, signaled a warning. It was going to be stormy. I have never experienced the eye of a cyclone, although we lived through some cyclone warnings in Queensland. The transition period, from leaving Australia until I took up my last position back in Finland, felt like the quiet center of a storm that was about to erupt. I knew it was going to come, and I realized it would be difficult. Should I wait until they fired me – which would happen if I continued to preach as I believed and not as the Church wanted me to? Or should I leave of my own free will? In the eye of a storm, there is no easy way out. This I soon came to realize.

During the weeks preceding my crucial meeting with the church council, I had discussions with my Bishop. During the three-hour drive to the Bishop's residence, my heart was beating rapidly in excitement. How would he react? How would I react? Would he try to convince me not to go through with it? Would I be strong enough to withstand the pressure? When I arrived, we were seated in the same salon where the reception on the eve of our ordination had taken place twelve years earlier. His wife served drinks and biscuits. I could tell that I was not the only one who was nervous. The Bishop realized there was a lot at stake, for him, his prestige and his Church. I explained my doubts about some of the Church's fundamental dogmas, which so greatly contrasted to what I had read in the Tanach. To me the Church had become just a large institution, no longer the Body of Christ. "Remember," the Bishop said to me, "you have to realize that you have a family to support. It will be very difficult out there for you if you leave the Church. You are responsible for the well-being of your family." I was shocked at his suggestion: "Let's keep quiet about what you really believe and you can keep your job." The biscuits almost stuck in my throat and my heart jumped. Did he really say what I thought he did? This kind of bargaining did not appeal to me and I left the Episcopal residence even more determined to give up my position, before they had a chance to fire me.

I went back to my office. It was located on the fourth floor. The whole building was part of a large complex that represented the might and power of the Lutheran Church in Finland. I felt almost guilty using the congregation's typewriter as I wrote a letter stating my decision to resign as minister of the Lutheran Church. Twelve years earlier I was solemnly ordained to the ministry, and now I was giving it up. I could not fight the Church, nor transform it. But I could leave. Slowly a feeling of freedom washed over me in the midst of all the chaos that was unfolding. My soul was about to be set free. I was elated, but at the same time, frightened. What was it like, living outside the Church? Could I survive or was it a freedom of death?

I called the Church council of my parish to a special session.

The meeting was about to begin, and we were all waiting – my wife, and I, the council of the parish, and the congregation that had only recently elected me as their minister. The Bishop called. He was going to be delayed. As we continued to wait, I thought back to the phone call I had received, telling me that I had been elected as the new minister of this congregation. I was in Australia at the time, and due to the different time zones, the call came at four o'clock in the morning. A few members of the congregation were phoning to congratulate me – I could hear their excitement at my election. With this in mind, I had mixed feelings to say the least. Was I betraying these people by leaving them after such a short time? Deep down, I knew there was much more at stake than the leadership of a parish. Within a short time, they would have a new minister, and would care little about what happened to me. It was certainly inconvenient for them, but not a catastrophe. As for me, I was risking my very existence, my faith, everything I had built my life upon. There was no turning back.

The Bishop finally arrived. Before the proceedings began, I handed him a plain envelope, which contained my letter of resignation. He was to take it to the Diocese, where it would either be accepted or rejected. Then, I opened the meeting, and asked to address the audience. In front of the entire congregation, I made the same statement as in the private meeting with my superior, the Bishop. With my Bible in hand, I pointed at the practices where, to my understanding, the Church had deviated from the clear meaning of the text. I explained that I could not find trinity in the Bible. Nor could I find Sunday as a day of rest. And I stated that in many practices the Church tried to imitate Judaism, while still opposing the Jewish people throughout history. I made it very clear that my loyalty would be to the Bible, as I understood it, and not to the Lutheran institution.

The longer I spoke, the greater the tension in the room. I could sense how uncomfortable the situation was for everyone present. Some tried to hide their feelings, while others could not. Those who did not succeed revealed a face that said it all. "How dare you challenge the infallible, holy Church?" Others in plain instinct of self-preservation pretended not to lower themselves by responding.

The Bishop did not interrupt me, although he looked nervous and angry. When I finished, after speaking for no more than thirty minutes, I expected there would be a discussion. There was none. After a short silence, the Bishop, his face white, and his body trembling with anger, did not hesitate. He pointed to the exit and said: "There is the door, I ask you to leave!" I was shocked. He repeated himself. Never before had I been thrown out of a meeting. I could not move. This time the Bishop tried to add more power to his statement: "According to Martin Luther you are a heretic. There is the door, I ask you to leave!"

I was ready to leave, but nevertheless, this came as a shock. My wife and I left the room. Another couple from the council joined us and expressed their support. Tears spilled from our eyes as we embraced, knowing that the moment had finally passed, and it had been unavoidable.

Suddenly my friend reminded me what the Bishop had just said. "Did you notice? He did not say 'you are a heretic according to the Bible,' but 'according to Martin Luther'?" I could live with that. That was exactly the support and comfort I needed at that moment. Although I was convinced that my actions were correct, the consequences were serious. I had a family – my wife and four daughters – to support. And I had just quit everything that I knew best – preaching, teaching, leading a congregation. Suddenly, all my skills and experience were worthless.

At that moment I also remembered a dream I had a few weeks earlier. In the dream I was at a meeting where something very important was going on. I stood up in my usual manner, and gave a talk on a subject very dear to me. I explained my position, expecting people to understand, and hopefully even to accept my arguments. But in the meeting, the majority went against me, and only a very few dared to take my side.

Until now, I had not paid very much attention to the dream, but now I saw that the meeting that had just taken place was the same as in my dream. This realization was like a fatherly pat on the shoulder telling me: "Just follow the script, this was all planned in advance." It did not necessarily make it easier, but I felt more confident that I was doing the right thing.

The storm was not over yet. Now came the journalists with their questions. During the next few days, all the main newspapers were filled with headlines about the Lutheran minister who quit the Church. But I not only left the ministry, I had to leave the Church altogether. I entered my office once again, this time to ask my secretary for the special form that would annul my membership of the Church.

I did not know what the future had in store for us. But did it matter? I was not seeking an easy way out, nor did I deliberately choose the difficult path. I followed my conscience and acted accordingly. I had strong faith in God, that He would somehow provide for our daily needs and give guidance towards a new life. My fear of God exceeded my fear of the institution. We left the Church not knowing that we would eventually convert to Judaism. This was our exodus. The future was unknown.

A week after the meeting, I received an answer from the Diocese. My resignation was accepted in a letter on a piece of paper as formal and solemn as my letter of ordination twelve years earlier, decorated with the insignia of the Church. The resignation took effect immediately with no remuneration. I had not expected any. The duties ended and so did the privileges. The financial benefits of monthly pay and a house in which to live were all gone in an instant. So too was the status of privilege.

Twelve years of service to the Church was over. I would not miss the institution, but I would certainly miss the people, the fellowship, and the work I so loved. Suddenly I was on my own. I could not decipher my feelings. Did I leave my congregation and my past life on shore, or was I the one who was left stranded? Either way it was clear – the people of the Church had their path, and I had mine. We were drifting apart – never to be united again.

SIX

New Awakenings

WHAT WERE the events that led up to this meeting? What took place within me during all those years as a minister? Why do I find myself where I am today? These questions are very important to me. Without them, I would not find any reason for having studied theology or becoming a minister. After all, if there were nothing enjoyable or meaningful about the ministry or the Church, if I had only miserable memories, then of course my leaving could be easily explained. Yet, this was not the case. Mostly I enjoyed being a minister and felt very comfortable with the challenges of the job. I did not leave because I disliked the job – I left despite my love for it.

For many years, I was completely satisfied with my career. There were no question marks on my choice of profession, no conflict in my heart. I was not outspoken during my school years and I am still not a pushy person; rather I am quite shy. Early on in my clerical career I found great satisfaction in public speaking and there were plenty of opportunities to channel enjoyment. In an informal setting I might take my time, carefully thinking about what I wish to say. Small talk is not my strong point. But give me a subject and a pulpit and I am challenged to capture the audience, large or small.

What does a minister actually do? His job is comparable to the duties of a rabbi or a teacher. I gave countless speeches at weddings and other ceremonies, and numerous lessons for confirmation classes. Of course the main event every week was the Sunday sermon. What to preach? That was a challenge – to say something that would inspire the congregation, nourish their souls. Not just cliches or dead letters, but something real. I felt comfortable in my position, and it suited me well. No wonder it was difficult for so many, especially for my closest relatives, to understand my resignation. I have some wonderful memories from my time as a minister.

*   *   *

The summer in Finland is short but intense, both in life and light. Everything has to happen during these few weeks, when there is almost nonstop daylight and the vegetation is lush as a fresh bowl of salad. I recall one particular summer when I was serving in a small parish, a fishing and farming community by the Baltic Sea on the Finnish West Coast. The population of this village doubled from one to two thousand during the vacation period. People flocked to their summer cottages and spent their free time by the sea, fishing, picking blueberries in the forests, steaming a sauna on Saturday night – that's Finland!

I had an idea: why not do something special? A music festival? Everybody was delighted. We managed to engage some popular gospel artists from Sweden. Our local choir could not compete, but never mind, it was not a competition. Their song was filled with the same joy as that of any artist. For me it was important to give something special to these people, a spiritual lift, a memory that would fill their souls with joy during the dark nights of the long, cold winter, when the sea was frozen and the visitors gone.

My good friend was a TV producer, with whom I had broadcasted several radio productions. The idea of a music festival grew to become a TV production broadcast in both Finland and Sweden. It was an outdoor event, and we were taking a risk – it could rain any day, without prior warning of more than a few hours. But it did not rain. It was a beautiful day.

The greater the event, the greater the excitement. As a preacher I felt like an artist. Preaching is a performance in which you have to capture the audience. But a preacher is also a guide. He takes you by the hand and leads you to a lookout, where he can show you something remarkable. That day, because of exposure in the media, I had a very large turnout. The idea of a music festival on a warm, sunny summer afternoon materialized into a tradition for the small parish, not always accompanied by TV cameras, but always filled with song, joy, and food for the soul.

*   *   *

Can anything beat the beauty of the Finnish summer? Just as the question crosses my mind, another memory appears to me. During our stay in Australia, my tiny office was situated in Greenslopes, Brisbane. The Finnish Lutheran Church, whose work in Australia began as a seaman's mission in the early twentieth century, was now located in a very insignificant house on Bunya Street. Our neighbor on one side was a Catholic chapel, and on the other side of the street, a few hundred meters south, there was a synagogue. The people who ran the corner shop were Jewish. When we arrived in Australia, Linda was seven and Sara five. The youngest, the twins, were only three. One day Josefin and Karolin, mostly just called "The Twins," decided to go for a "walkabout" in Greenslopes. When Runa realized they were gone, she frantically searched for them. At the corner shop, there stood Moshe, the owner of the store, pointing after Karolin in one direction, and Father Ralph, the Catholic priest, pointing after Josefin in the opposite direction. I ran out of my office to help my wife in the search. The adventure ended without mishap. Moshe, himself a father of five, was still smiling at us when we returned with the girls, while Father Ralph sighed in relief that he did not have the trouble of kids.

*   *   *

One day in my office, the phone rang loudly. This time it was a Swedish couple that wanted to get married. We decided to meet to discuss the important event. It appeared that they had made great preparations to ensure a memorable wedding. When they arrived they handed me an airline ticket to the Great Barrier Reef. The wedding was to take place on a yacht sailing out to the reef. At the wedding, I heard many appreciative comments. "What a yacht!" "What a reef!" My comment was: "What a wedding!" We were surrounded by warm, turquoise water. In the background, just a mile away, we could see a tropical island with sandy beaches and palm trees. On the top deck of the yacht, under the protective shade, the visitors were beautifully dressed for the occasion. The bride and bridegroom came up from the lower deck for the ceremony, which was to take place just behind the captain's deck and huge steering wheel.

During the ceremony, I spoke about the commitment of marriage, how important it is to be partners and friends, allowing mutual love to grow. The couple exchanged rings and the musicians played a soft wedding march. Then, as if orchestrated for the scene by the ultimate wedding host, pairs of dolphins began to encircle the yacht. It is often said that dolphins are like humans, but this was extraordinary! Dolphins are sometimes sighted swimming in pairs, and it is said that the male and female stay together for a lifetime. The beautiful message of the dolphins definitely beat my speech.

*   *   *

The question remains for me to ponder: why? Why give it all up, despite a profession that was interesting and promising? How could I expect my family to cope with all the changes and new challenges? These questions followed me for many years, because the changes I had made in our lives were demanding too much – and what are we but human? But there has to be something more. We must look deeper than the human part of ourselves, deeper than the material aspects of life. We must search for the satisfaction of the soul. Our soul connects us to the spiritual world and our Creator. If this connection is not tuned in, we crave something more. We must discover a depth, which does not readily reveal itself to us. I believe it is our duty to explore life and to ensure we do not starve our souls in favor of the more visible aspects of life.

SEVEN

In the Public Eye

THE MORNING AFTER the church council meeting was unlike any other. For the first time in my life, I was not a member of the Church. For the first time, I was unemployed. Suddenly I had no position, no authority, no office – no salary. Soon I would not even have a house to live in. What a freedom!

Perhaps I never felt "trapped," but nevertheless, the morning after that meeting, I felt as if I had been released from twelve years of a well-organized life. But suddenly the question struck me: freedom to what end? How long would the lonely walk in the desert last? What about basic needs, such as food and shelter?

Certainly I could believe what I wanted, but for the moment I was formally without a religion. If it was difficult for me, it seemed to be even more problematic to others. They did not know how to label me; I could not be connected to any denomination. The newspapers printed huge headlines: "MINISTER LEAVES MINISTRY AND THE CHURCH." But how could they handle me when they couldn't quite grasp me? I found myself outside the framework of accepted belief. The press treated me as a traveler who is suddenly found without a passport. I was unidentifiable.

The question of my identity was crucial for me on a personal level. Who am I? What is the state of my soul? "Without the Church – no salvation." This is a more Catholic than Protestant statement, but still a very common belief in the Christian world.

The importance of religion as part of one's identity became very clear to me during this experience. I'm not talking about the level of observance.

Even a person who is not observant, whether Christian or Jewish, knows what religion he belongs to. No longer members of any faith, we were without a fellowship, without anybody to worship with, without holidays. We had stopped celebrating Christmas and Easter but had not yet gained Hanukka or Passover. What calendar should we follow? The only days we celebrated were our own birthdays. Without religion there is nobody to bless a newborn baby or to bury your dead. There is more to religion than you think. You realize this all the more when you don't have it.

In the aftermath of our departure from the Church we never met with any blatant hostility, but we certainly had a feeling of being frozen out. "We don't understand why you left, so if life is hard for you, it's your own fault." The soft criticism hovered quietly in the air. The press in Finland can at times be nasty to its own people, but when it comes to closing ranks against a heretic, they certainly side with their own. Besides the whisperings, we were confronted by a death-like silence. Nobody stopped to ask us about our departure, nobody wanted to talk about it. We found ourselves in a state of mourning, psychological mourning for our former life.

In contrast to this, it felt good to know that there were a few who did not hide their support. Among them was the young couple that left the Church together with us, and two other longtime friends of Israel. Their support made it easier to get through this difficult time.

Amongst themselves, my relatives asked what had happened. I felt obligated to tell them my side of the story. Otherwise they would have to rely only on the writings of the journalists, and these were not always favorable, to say the least. I placed a small ad in the local newspaper of my hometown calling relatives and those who were interested to listen to my reasoning. The topic of my talk, to quote the rumor, was "What's wrong with Ole?" I assumed that my relatives would not agree with my explanations, but still I preferred to tell them in person, rather than leave it open to speculation.

I no longer had any obligations on Sundays. In the church, Sundays were the busiest day of my week, with Church services and a variety of ceremonies at which to officiate. It was a Sunday when we made the three-hour drive to Kronoby, where I had rented the local communal hall for the occasion.

Kronoby is the home of my wife's family and the neighboring municipality of my hometown, Karleby. In Kronoby we had always felt welcome, because Runa's old childhood home was waiting for our visits. Runa's father died before she was born, and her mother Karin passed away only a year after my ordination. Blessed be her memory. She was a warm-hearted, wonderful mother-in-law. Runa has a brother, John, and a sister, Eva-Maj, in Finland, two brothers, Sigward and Bill, living in Sweden, and a sister, Gunlis, in Australia. Many relatives from both sides of the family came to listen to my story, some of whom we had not seen for years. Cousins, aunts and uncles, friends, former colleagues, and neighbors. My sister and brother also came, but not Birger, who was a minister himself. Of course I did not expect him to attend, as he was living in neighboring Sweden, but the fact that I was declaring my reasons for leaving Christianity did not help matters.

Two years earlier, while we still were in Australia, my mother, blessed be her memory, passed away. I remember my parents with warmth and love. So when I looked at the expressions on my family's faces, I knew what they were thinking. My sister and my aunt looked serious and sad. "You are thinking about Mom Linnea," I said, when I greeted them. "Yes, what would she have said about all this? Are you glad she didn't need to be here today to hear this?" My aunt nodded reluctantly, too embarrassed to agree verbally.

I deeply respected my parents, in spite of the fact that I took actions against their faith and way of living. But the upbringing they gave me, which nurtured my respect for the Torah, leads me to believe that, had they been present, they would have been the most understanding of all. I felt some of this sympathy from my eldest brother, who was also quite critical of the established Church, although he never left it. Yet, in agreement with my aunt, I comforted myself with the thought that my parents didn't have to attend this meeting.

The hall was packed. It was not a private family affair anymore. This was also the hometown of the Bishop who had ordained me and his brother who had just dismissed me. The elder of the Episcopal brothers was now the Archbishop of Finland, so it was indeed a daring task, to rebel against the Church in this very town. The Episcopal brothers and their families were very respected and influential, not only amongst the local community but the entire population.

The meeting was not an attempt on my part to preach to my relatives; I would not have succeeded anyway. In a country with freedom of religion

and speech, I simply wanted to express my view on the factors that had
led to my resignation. Of course, this could not happen without defense
from the institutional side. Some Church ministers also sat in the audience
to give moral support to their parishioners. However the support was not
only moral, taking a clear verbal form as well. Legally there is freedom of
religion in Finland, but with the vast majority of the population belonging
to the Lutheran State Church, the moral pressure to stay with the majority is very strong. There are two official Churches, the Lutheran and the
Greek Orthodox. Each has official status and collects tax money from their
members through the state taxation system. Then there are several free
denominations like the Pentecostals and Baptists and others.

"How could you place yourself outside the Body of Christ?" a former
colleague, a minister in the Church, asked. The meaning was crystal clear.
What he actually meant was: "You have doomed yourself to hell." To have
faith is very important; to share the faith with the Church is the most
important thing for the people inside. For me to explain that I did not lose
my faith, rather I just did not believe as the Church did, was too hard for
him, and many others, to comprehend.

During my speech, every now and then, I could hear a soft "amen"
from somebody agreeing on a certain issue. Of course this was encouraging
for me – it was not completely enemy territory after all. But most of my
relatives strongly voiced their disagreement without letting it affect our
personal relations. "Remember, you are welcome to our house as always
before," my aunt said to me with tears in her eyes, when she hugged me
after the meeting. That was, after all, the most common reaction. They
respected me for what I had done although they did not agree. I was satisfied with the outcome. I could return home and continue my life and enjoy
my newly-won freedom.

We were still living in the apartment provided by the congregation,
a privilege we had enjoyed during all the ministerial years. Sometimes
the house provided was a real mansion, like those so often seen in the
countryside in Finland. The typical vicarage was yellow with white boards
on the corners of the house and around the windows. Yellow is a common
color for mansions while the typical country-style house is mostly red.
Among ministers, the vicarage was still not very popular, which was hard
for the parish members, who often looked with envy on those mansions, to
believe. The reason that they were not popular was for economic reasons.

Although provided by the congregation, the inhabitants had to pay tax on the square meters they occupied. This often ended up being more than the equivalent rent for a similar home. Often the minister had to fight for the right to move out on his own, rather than stay in the house provided for him. Now came our time to move out. Our fight of a different kind was over, our bond with the Church came to an end, and we did not even want to continue living as tenants with the Church as our landlord. We were still allowed to stay for a limited period, but we chose not to.

Before we had time to worry too much about our future livelihood, we rented a house, still in Tampere. I recall thinking that this could not go on for very long. The Bishop's words about my responsibility to support my family buzzed in my head. What am I going to do? I must admit that I expected it to be easier to find employment after leaving the Church than it turned out to be. "Look, there he is." The eyes of those who saw me as an outcast followed me everywhere. With this attitude, in a country in which eighty percent of the population belongs to the Lutheran Church, it was not easy to feel confident. "Blame only yourself, you had everything you could have wished for, but you threw it all overboard." Nobody said it directly to me, but a well-trained, sensitive ear heard the words anyway.

I tried teaching, journalism, advertising; I applied to every possible job listed in the vacancy section, with no luck. In a desperate last attempt to take some positive action, we set up our own business. Or should I say, my wife started her design business, with me as her assistant. She had studied interior design, with furniture design as her specialty, at the Queensland College of Art in Brisbane. She was very eager to make her first collection of design furniture. Investing our savings in this business we started what we thought could become a new life career. We produced some beautiful pieces of furniture, even selling abroad, but the business never took off as planned. The early 1990s saw economic depression in Finland, which made it almost impossible to succeed in a newly established business. Realizing we had made a mistake, we comforted ourselves with the fact that we had no choice but to try. That consolation did not help much when it came to putting food on the table. We had to take action, and get on with our lives.

"Why not move to your hometown, where life might be easier after all?" This suggestion from our friends Tellervo and Helena, who tried to help us, came at a critical time.

So we packed our belongings once again. This time the move was within Finland, but still a difficult one for many reasons. Neither my wife nor I had a job. Our daughters had to change school once again. We couldn't increase our income, so we tried at least to lower our expenses. In our hometown, housing costs were much lower. We hoped that this move would bring us stability that we so badly needed.

EIGHT

No Man's Land

THIS WAS A time without a religion. On the one hand, we were engaged in a battle to find a spiritual home that could nourish the soul. What if we could not find an answer to this longing in our new environment? The ongoing search made us feel restless. A state of emptiness and alienation pulled us in one direction. On the other hand, we had to stay and concentrate on a new career and school for the girls until we knew what we were going to do next.

Coming home to Kronoby did not automatically make it any easier to find employment. Looking for a job in this area was more comfortable, since we had more contacts and knew more people, but I was still the ex-minister with a degree in theology that was not even good enough to teach religion in schools. Even a schoolteacher of religion must be approved by the Church. My first job was as a part-time English teacher for an institute of adult education. It was an enormous relief to find this position, because by that time I had been unemployed for almost two years, the most difficult period of my life.

With this part-time job I slowly got myself back on track, gaining self-confidence. I was needed. My talents could be used again. I enjoyed the classes and the response from the students told me that the feeling was mutual.

Not only did the job do me good, but it also sent a clear message to the community where we lived. "He is a decent fellow after all." I had started to regain lost confidence. It took time, but I was on my way. My teaching hours were increased and by the next school year I was offered a full-time position in an elementary school. I always regarded teaching as one of my favorite occupations, and I was looking forward to this new position. Although I prefer teaching adults, or at least teenagers, I was eager to get started and did not care that this was a fifth-grade class. Many aspects of the job were new to me. I had to teach Mathematics, Biology, Woodwork, Gymnastics, English, and Civics, but not Religion – the only subject in which I had formal qualifications. I enjoyed it anyway. For me it was a great challenge to ensure that these children were actually learning, not just attending school each day. As a minister, I had loved teaching and interacting with people. The same applied to this job. I loved teaching and I loved the children.

My job prospects for the next school year were not promising. The school had to decrease the number of teachers, and I was let go. Before I had time to make any new plans, I received a phone call from the director of education. He offered me another teaching position at a special school for "problem teenagers." Difficult situations and new tasks always challenged me, so this was definitely something that interested me. Since the director had watched me in action as a teacher, and had enough faith in me to offer me the job, I felt confident enough to accept it. Again I faced a completely new situation. This school, called Lagmansgarden, was beautifully located in the typical flat West Coast landscape, accommodated in a gorgeous old mansion surrounded by large fields and park-like forests. The school had its own tennis court and sports field, although the number of students did not even make up one football team. The school aimed to provide tranquility and harmony for the youngsters, who often came from backgrounds of drug abuse and broken homes.

The teaching was almost on a one-to-one basis, since classes consisted of only four to six students. I made a point of getting to know my students, gaining their confidence and communicating with them. This was no easy task, as so many of them had extremely bad experiences with adults. During this time I also came to know and respect some experienced professionals in the field of treating drug addiction. Some of the educational methods included long walks in the Finnish Lappland. Hikes of ten to twenty miles per day for one week in the wilderness made the tough guys soft and malleable, and more receptive to influence than they had been in years. I used to think that we should take their parents on similar hikes as well, since so often the problems were mirror images of what they had seen at home in their parents – those who had any.

The place we called home during our time in Kronoby was Runa's childhood home. It was an old farmhouse called The Tailor's or "Skraddas" in Swedish, because her grandfather used to be a tailor. Runa's father was a farmer with a special interest in horses. He had been a jockey and won many races with his favorite horse, Fonte.

One warm spring afternoon my wife and I were sitting in the south corner at The Tailor's, drinking coffee and eating freshly baked wheat buns. Gloria, our golden retriever, was playfully running around, picking up the stick we threw for her. She was Sara's dog; Sara loves animals and nature and Gloria was the ideal companion for her. Often they went to the forest for long walks. Now I understand the saying that the owner so often resembles their pet. Sara was as blond as Gloria, or vice versa.

From a distance I could see our neighbor approaching. He was our city councilor and this year was election year. I had a funny feeling that I knew what he had in mind and already started to think how I would answer him. It took him some time to get to the point. He joined us for coffee and the discussion consisted mostly of talk about the weather and the approaching agricultural season. The growing season in this part of Finland is short but intense. The long hours of daylight during summer make up for the short season. Finland's location on the map does not give a correct picture of her climate. The altitude might be the same as Alaska, but due to the Gulf Stream that brings warm air from the Atlantic Ocean, the summer can be rather pleasant. Finland's main crops are barley, rye, wheat, and oats, and, of course, potato.

Our neighbor was a farmer, known to be very knowledgeable and intelligent. Not many of his generation spoke English, but Torolf had studied on his own and often had to function as a translator when somebody in the village received a letter from a relative who emigrated to the United States generations ago. Almost every family had somebody who had emigrated "over there." Runa's three uncles left for Canada in the 1930s.

I was enjoying our coffee and chat, but I was curious about the real reason for Torolf's visit. Finally he came to the point. My suspicions were confirmed. He asked me if I was prepared to be a candidate at the upcoming election in the municipal council. Communal affairs and politics interested me, along with many other things. I was attracted to the idea. There was only one big question mark. I needed votes to be elected. Who would vote for me? Every single voter in the entire district belonged to the Church, and even if the city council did not have anything to do with religious affairs, there was still a dividing line between me and the electorate. Torolf was not particularly religious, so he did not place too much emphasis on my decision to leave the Church. "Don't worry about that," he said, "people here know you. I have asked around and many agree that you will have the support needed to get in." Ask again, I begged him. I also needed time to reflect on the idea myself. Who said I was going to stay in Kronoby for the next four years, the duration of the mandate?

Choices can only be made against the background of existing options. For the moment we did not have any other option but to stay in our small hometown. My decision was made easier by this realization. I have always wanted to fill my life to the brim with meaning and quality. If I could contribute to our community, and be a representative of the people in my region at the same time, I'd be happy to give it a go. When Torolf came the next time, he didn't need to persuade me. I was ready to accept candidacy.

Election Day drew near. There was tension in the air and butterflies in my stomach. The campaign leading up to the event threw me into a whole world of new engagements. I had to enroll as member of a political party. Suddenly I found myself in an environment very much to my liking. Meetings, debates, and public appearances were all part of my past, and now I could use my experiences in a meaningful way, instead of letting it all go to waste.

The polling booths closed and counting of votes began. My neighbor was right. I got the support from a majority of voters in my district, which entitled me to membership in our municipal council. It was not a full-time job. Neither was it well paid, but the big issue for me was my growing confidence. The people seemed to have set aside our differences. The election result proved that my neighbors were surprisingly open-minded, and this knowledge strengthened my resolve to work for the community. The term was for four years. I was a little frightened by the length of the commitment – our constant spiritual search could lead us somewhere else before the term was complete. Once again, I decided I must choose between existing alternatives. So we concentrated on the present situation and continued with our life to the best of our ability. During my time as a councilor I was a member of the educational board and before the termination of the period, I became vice president of the council.

There are many layers to a personality and many aspects to the identity of a soul. On a spiritual and religious level, I had no identity. I was looking deep into myself, asking, what is the state of my soul? The Divine power that gave me my soul when I was created – what stamp did He put on it? I felt as if I had found an old coin, and was turning it over carefully in my hand, trying to decipher any marks on it to identify its origins. What value did it have and more important, where did it come from and to whom did it belong? And furthermore, how could it best fulfill its function, not to be wasted or lost, but used exactly for its purpose? Because the One Who created it did so for a purpose.

These questions filled my entire being, day and night. I could have left everything, at any time, just to seek the answers to these questions, if I only knew where to go or how to search. The only words that came to me again and again were: with no options you cannot choose. For us this meant staying where we were for the time being. And making the best of what we had. So despite a spiritual struggle and religious questioning that left me very dissatisfied, we stayed and filled our life with work and engagements until another option presented itself in an unknown future. Luckily, as the municipal election proved, my professional prospects were improving, and we were settling into a normal routine.

Through my duties as a city councilor, I came into contact with interesting organizations and potential employers. For a while I had directed my thoughts towards a certain high school that was in need of a headmaster. One day, when I was teaching at Lagmansgarden's Special School, I received a phone call from the acting headmaster of Kronoby Folk High School. I was fairly certain I knew what he was going to ask me, or rather I so badly hoped to hear the question that I knew it already. In any case, the question came. "Are you prepared to take up the position as our headmaster?" A Folk High School is an educational institute for adults. Its origin is Danish and many of the Folk High Schools in Scandinavia are established and supported by Christian organizations, but not this one. That suited me very well. I agreed to meet the directors of the school the following week. They did not want to waste any time and neither did I. The new position was to commence within a few weeks.

Becoming a headmaster was like a dream come true. I agreed to start as principal and headmaster for Kronoby Folk High School, supported by several municipalities in the region. Here I could channel all my talents and develop new ones. I hadn't enjoyed a job as much as this in a long time. The school organized different courses within a wide variety of fields from Information Technology and Handicrafts, to Personal Development and Wilderness Guide Instruction. As part of the new job, I studied creative thinking, which I later developed into lectures for different professional groups within the framework of the school program. These courses gained popularity and we had municipality workers, teachers, taxation officers, hospital workers, and groups of unemployed people attending the seminars. If ever I derived a certain sense of satisfaction after a sermon, this sense of achievement was pale in comparison to my pleasure at the outcome and feedback from these lectures and workshops. I saw my task at the school as not just to lecture and develop the curriculum, but to facilitate communication among students and teachers. The atmosphere in a school is a reflection of the principal's office. Therefore my challenge was to achieve a strong morale and effective communication among my staff and students.

Looking at the "non-spiritual" side of life, we were very settled. Slowly but surely I had regained the confidence I lost in leaving the Church. By now I was my usual self again. I had a very satisfying and demanding job, engagements in politics and the community – more than I could take on. But I had a nagging feeling that something was missing. Life is more – much more! And I knew that. But until I could see clearly what my next move was, I had no choice but to stay on.

During those years I had learned that no matter how satisfying a job or fulfilling life seems to be on the surface, unless you are in harmony with your soul, you will have a constant feeling that something is missing. That was how I felt. I flipped my old coin again, and still I could not find any engravings on it. I had no place to deposit my finding. Nobody would accept it, nobody knew its value. Was it only a rusty piece of metal? I was scratching and cleaning it, hoping to find the engravings that would reveal its origin and value. It was precious to me, so I kept it carefully until the day when the original engravings would shine through.

NINE

Strangers in Our Own Land

"We are strangers in our own land." This said it all. We could not deny our dissatisfaction with our spiritual situation. We were slowly settling into a secure position with work and commitments. But deep inside, something else was happening. We began to feel drawn to everything Jewish. Just seeing a Jewish book in the library, or the Star of David, stirred our emotions and made us feel a longing for something unfamiliar. We did not know any Jews in Finland. The only Jews we had met were visitors from Israel, who were introduced to us by our friends. Like a magnet to metal, we were being pulled in the direction of Judaism and of *Eretz Yisrael*. My wife and I traveled to the Israeli Embassy in Helsinki to enquire about emigration to Israel. The Embassy received us very politely, and while we were still talking to the embassy personnel, the news reached the ambassador that there were crazy Finns in the embassy who wanted to move to Israel. Obviously feeling amused and curious, he invited us to his office for a friendly talk to find out for himself what was going on.

During our casual talk, I referred to the Tanach, where it states that even strangers one day will come and ask the Jews for permission to walk with them to the Holy Mountain and settle the Land (Isaiah 56:6–7, Amos 9:11–15). The ambassador appreciated the biblical references, but was more interested in practicalities. "How will you be able to cope with the huge differences in the culture? And what about the people, they are not as nice as Scandinavians, and the food, imagine if you don't like the Israeli falafel or hummus and the hot climate?" Not one of his points scared us. So what? We will love the people, we love spicy food, and we would rather be without

59

the cold climate. As his position demands, he was very professional and diplomatic, and he left us with the feeling that if it were up to him alone, he would gladly let us immigrate immediately. We couldn't be disappointed in him. But there were obstacles in the way; one of them was that we had not yet converted. We had known in advance that this may be a problem, but we also realized that this was a door that we might need to knock on many times before it would open, so we figured we had better start knocking.

We felt a strange pull to *Eretz Yisrael*, as a magnet pulls metal. The pulling power is invisible but real. Yet it works the opposite way too. If you turn the magnet around, there is a push, a rejection. We also felt this push. Every week, there was the conflict between Shabbat and Sunday. We had to live through the holidays but could no longer share them. More and more, our food took on a foreign taste in our mouths.

We were like an implant in a foreign body and were about to be rejected because there were too many factors preventing us from fitting in. We became very sensitive to imitators and pretenders in the world of religion. We did not leave a false church to join yet another false denomination. Therefore we were digging deep. The fact that the Bible talks about how strangers and foreigners in the future will join the Jewish people and walk on the soil of *Eretz Yisrael* was for us an assertion that we could seriously approach the Jewish religion and even make a claim to come and live in the land promised to the Jews.

We had already moved around the world twice. This was actually an advantage for us. We already knew what was involved. We were not deeply rooted in Finland. Besides, we all liked travelling, especially the girls. But moving the whole family to another country involves more than just an airplane flight. So I had to ask myself, how many times can you replant a tree? Is one more time too much, or will it survive another uprooting? Will the girls be able to cope? For my wife and myself, there was this strange connection, the pull in the direction towards Israel. I was not as worried about us as I was about our daughters. Runa and I totally agreed on the importance of making *aliyah*. We could argue about the trivialities, but when it came to the large issues, such as our faith and Israel, we never disagreed. If I was strongly opinionated, so was she. Runa was not only supporting me during this process, she was actively seeking her own progress, constantly praying and learning. Yet, doesn't a young plant take root more easily than an older one? So maybe I shouldn't worry about our daughters, as much as about myself?

Kronoby is a long distance from any Jewish community. To my knowledge there is not a single Jew in Kronoby. The drive to Helsinki, with its Jewish population of less than 2,000, takes about five hours. At that time, Helsinki did not have a rabbi, although it had a very active community. So the congregation in Helsinki referred me to the rabbi in Stockholm. If Helsinki was far away, Stockholm was even further. I contacted the rabbi in writing. He answered me in a friendly manner, but our request for conversion was rejected. He explained how difficult it would be and how heavy the burden of the commitments would be compared to what I was used to. I was disappointed but I did not give up.

On one of my political engagements, I traveled to Stockholm and took the opportunity to visit the synagogue and meet the rabbi. I arrived by boat. Finns are spoiled with large ships traveling between the two Nordic countries. These floating luxury hotels journey through the world's second largest archipelago, next only in size to the Greek archipelago. I walked all the way from the port to the synagogue. When I arrived, it was time for the evening prayer. For some time, I knocked at the door and nobody answered, until I realized that the synagogue used another entrance. I was knocking at the wrong door. How hard it was to find the right door for conversion! I did not know then that prospective converts are usually rejected at first. After this meeting in person, the rabbi appreciated my situation and we engaged in dialogue. Later, when a rabbi was appointed in Helsinki, I was referred to him and continued my contacts closer to home.

Throughout this period, we felt we were living a shadowy existence. First and foremost we had our everyday lives, filled with work, livelihood, commitments and responsibilities. At the same time we did not spare any opportunity to pursue our spiritual goal. We did this quietly, not exactly in secret, but without any demonstrative fuss. During one of my business trips to Helsinki, which I took with a colleague from school, I needed to visit the Israeli Embassy. Since I was about to take on some new work commitments, I did not want to reveal to my colleague that I had other reasons for going to the Israeli Embassy. I could not lie, but did not reveal the whole truth either, so I explained that we wanted to manufacture my wife's furniture designs in Israel. My appointment was with the commercial attaché. I did meet with him, but that was not my only contact at the embassy. My colleague betrayed a questioning look, but it was the end of our discussion, and he caught the train, while I turned towards the Embassy.

I once heard a story about a farmer and his poultry farm. The story did not make any sense to me until I converted to Judaism. An eagle egg was mistakenly placed among the eggs that a mother hen was sitting on. The day arrived when the chicks stuck their tiny beaks through the egg and wanted to see daylight. So too did the little eagle. This baby eagle grew up together with the hens on the farm. At first the young eagle did not realize it was any different from the other inhabitants of the place. It tried to pick the grain from the ground as did the other birds, but it seemed to be so difficult to eat the same food. It started to act differently and behave strangely and feel more and more uncomfortable surrounded by the hens.

Meanwhile the mother eagle also realized that one of her young ones was missing. She started to fly around, calling from above, hoping that her missing young bird would respond to her call. One day the young eagle heard the voice of his mother calling. It was a new voice, but still it was familiar. The young eagle tried his wings and flew up to follow his mother. Finally he realized: "I'm not a chicken, I'm an eagle."

I was still bothered by the question of the identity of my soul. In the Jewish faith we learn that the soul is divine, that it is created separately to the body and nourishes the body. It is only during our lifetime that the soul and the body are connected. Unlike other religions, which hold that man is born with a sinful soul, Judaism maintains that every Jew is born with a pure soul free from sin. Our soul is eternal. It existed before it came to live in our body and will continue to exist after the body dies.

I was born in Finland to Christian parents, but what kind of soul did God give me? Was there a mistake in the giving of souls? Maybe the angel taking care of "soul deliveries" mixed up the address. Instead of giving my soul to a Bachmann or Brenner in Carmiel he delivered it to a Brunell in Karleby, Finland. And what about Runa? The same thing must have happened to her. Yet God has a better "delivery record" than that. No mistakes from His side. The answer must be found elsewhere.

There is a Midrash (Bible commentary) which states that God, before offering the Torah to the Jews, went to all the other nations with the same offer. None of them were willing to accept the difficult rules and regulations as a nation, but among them were individuals who stood on their tiptoes waving frantically to capture God's attention, expressing their willingness to accept the Torah. When God gave the Torah to His people at Mt. Sinai, the souls of the converts were also present, those who so eagerly wanted to accept the Torah as their own.

Rabbi Josef Lifland in his book *Converts and Conversions* presents a different, very interesting comment on the souls of the converts at Mt. Sinai. Moshe tells the people: "Not with you alone do I make this covenant…with those who are standing here with us this day…and also those who are not here with us" (Deuteronomy 29:13–14). So if the covenant was made with people who were not present, how were they represented at Mt. Sinai? According to Rabbi Lifland the souls of all Jews were present, but not of converts. He explains, "The difference between a Jew's relationship with the revelation at Sinai and that of a convert is that every Jew of every generation was present when the Torah was given, if not in body at least in soul. The convert, on the other hand, was there neither in body nor in soul – only his '*mazal*' (destiny) was present." According to Rabbi Lifland, in order to understand this, we must realize that there are higher elements of spirituality to the human being, in addition to his soul that is "attached" to the body. These higher elements, which are not "attached" to the body, heard the voice going forth from Mt. Sinai. It is because of his *mazal*, for example, that one may suddenly have thoughts of repentance. These thoughts stem from a realm beyond consciousness. *Mazal* is the influence that flows from above into the soul.

Jews believe that one day all nations will recognize God's sovereignty and submit themselves to Him. The thoughts that will bring them to this state will come from their *mazal*. The true proselyte, says Rabbi Lifland, is one who comes to this recognition earlier than the rest of the world, and because of this he merits shelter under the wings of the Divine presence. All this is a result of his *mazal* having stood upon Mt. Sinai.

Why did the Almighty place my soul in a body that happened to be born in Finland to Christian parents? If I exclude the possibility of a mistake, since I don't believe that God makes mistakes, I have to continue my search. But the fact is, at that time, I felt very much like the young eagle bird. We did not want to eat the food. We became vegetarians. We behaved differently; we could not participate in the Christian holidays. When the Finns celebrated their festivals, we stayed home, and when we had Jewish festivals nobody celebrated. During these years we also learned the importance of the Christmas tree as a Christian folk symbol. For our relatives and neighbors, it was most upsetting when we stopped having the tree and celebrating Christmas. It became more and more obvious that we belonged elsewhere, and could not stay here; at least, not in our town, without a Jewish community. This was our call, and we had to answer it.

The girls, approaching their teens, had their own thoughts and were growing in faith in their own way. They heard our discussions at home and learned from what they saw in us. Parental example is often the best educational tool. It can also be helpful to use the power of persuasion – in moderation. Sometimes we had to pull hard to get to that point, but we never crossed the line. Being a parent is a difficult balancing trick. Often it is necessary to be soft and hard at the same time. Children need guidelines, but they also need an attentive ear, understanding, and love.

Often, in our many difficult decisions, we explained to our children our beliefs and what we were going to do, but the ultimate decision was theirs. To our great joy they too have arrived at the same conclusions, and followed in the same decisions.

Still pondering the identity of my soul – a pursuit that might take a lifetime – the secret written in my name was about to be revealed. When I was born, and the angels, whether mistaken or not, had delivered the soul, my mother said to my Godmother: "His name is to be Ole." What was the meaning of this name? Nobody could provide an answer. Nobody in the family had ever had such a name before me. My older siblings had names beginning with the letter *B*. Borje, Berit, Birger, and then, suddenly, Ole. It made no sense. Why not a name beginning with *B* for the youngest child?

It took me forty years to uncover the meaning of my name. During these years, when we tried to make the best of our situation, we worked hard in our shadow-like existence to come to terms with our longing for Israel and our attachment to the Jews. There was no family connection to a Jewish ancestor, at least not one that we could prove. But we wanted to create a connection; that is, to convert. During the initial stages of our conversion process, we began reading books about *aliyah*. There was constant mention of the "*Oleh*." This confused me until I found a translation for the word. Suddenly my name was explained. I had found its meaning. One who makes *aliyah* is an Oleh; and Ole, that was me. The literal meaning is "one who goes up." Without knowing it, my parents gave me the name

Ole – who was to go up to Israel, to one day become an *Oleh Hadash*. My conversion to Judaism was my *aliyah* to *Am Yisrael*, and my second aliyah was my immigration to *Eretz Yisrael*. The secret was hidden all these years. Nobody could provide a satisfying explanation until I was about to take the step that was already written in my name.

Ole Brunell and the Folk High School where he was a headmaster before making aliyah to Israel

TEN

Hear O Israel

I DID NOT SEE flashing lights, nor did I hear loud thunder, but along the way, over and over again, I heard a whispering in the wind: *Shema Yisrael, Adonai Eloheinu, Adonai Echad.*

Runa and I studied the Tanach together and found many passages that discussed how strangers and foreigners join with the Lord, God of Israel. These verses were calling to me: "This is the time, this is for you."

The Tanach talks about foreigners who have come to love the name of Hashem, who keep the Shabbat, and want to be His servants. Zecharia states (2:10): "Shout and be glad, O daughter of Zion, for I am coming and I will live among you, declares the Lord. Many nations will be joined with the Lord on that day and will become My people."

And Isaiah, the prophet says: "Also the sons of the strangers that join themselves to the Lord, to serve Him and to love the name of the Lord, to be His servants, everyone that keepeth the Shabbat from polluting it and taketh hold of My covenant. Even them will I bring to My Holy Mountain and make them joyful in My house of prayer" (Isaiah 56:6–7).

Another of those whispers was Zecharia, saying: "This is what the Lord Almighty says, 'Many peoples and the inhabitants of many cities will yet come and the inhabitants of one city will go to another and say, "Let us go at once to entreat the Lord Almighty. I myself am going." And many peoples and powerful nations will come to Jerusalem to seek the Lord Almighty and to entreat him.' This is what the Lord Almighty says: In those days ten men from all languages and nations will take firm hold of one Jew by the hem of his robe and say, 'Let us go with you, because we have heard that God is with you.'" (Zecharia 8:20–23).

There I was in a distant land, a foreigner, with my longing for the God of Israel, for His people and His land. He proclaims: also foreigners, also strangers will come. They will join in with the people, they will keep the Shabbat, they will take hold of the *tzitzit* (a four-cornered garment with fringes) of a Jew, to follow him, to ask him to teach them about their ways and the miracles of Hashem. How could I make it happen? What actions did I need to take to make it real for me?

Finally the Jewish congregation in Helsinki got their rabbi. I contacted him with the references from the rabbi in Stockholm. Once again, I took the opportunity, while in Helsinki on professional obligations, to contact Rabbi Michael Alony, the new rabbi there. At first he was busy, but I did not give up. I briefly introduced myself over the phone and urged him to give me at least fifteen minutes while I was in the capital. Over the phone he tried to convince me not to go ahead with my plans. He even added: "And for you it will also hurt." In his warning, I could already feel the *Mohel's* (person who performs the circumcision) knife on my skin, as I contemplated the circumcision I would have to undergo. But still I did not relent. I knew I was inching closer to finally getting the long process of converting underway. I was extremely determined – the rabbi could have asked me to meet him on top of Mount Everest and I would have. "Ok, come at two o'clock, but I have other commitments so I can only see you for a few minutes." Half an hour later, I entered his office at Malmgatan 26 in Helsinki, where the synagogue and the Jewish school were also located.

I felt totally vulnerable in this new environment. I did not know how to behave. I asked for Rabbi Michael Alony and was told to wait in the study hall. I explored his collection of books, mostly written in Hebrew, and let my fingers feel their covers, wishing that I could read and learn from these sources.

The rabbi greeted me warmly. Finally I felt I had an opportunity to share with someone my situation, my desires and my goals. I spoke from the very depths of my being, in a way I hadn't been able to do in a long time. To my great joy the rabbi listened. He had told me he was busy, and maybe he was, but we sat for one hour, two hours. I told him about the inner whisperings that urged me to join the Jewish people and move to Israel.

I leaned forward to get his attention. I had waited for this moment for a long time. Finally I could tell a rabbi, somebody who could help me, how I felt inside. Now it was just my soul talking. "We have left the 'Sunday-people' in order to join the 'Shabbat-people.' We have left the Trinity religion to be joined to the One and Only God of Israel. We have left the 'pork-eating' people to join the 'kosher-people.' We have left the people who celebrate pagan holidays in favor of the people who find their joy in the biblical holidays."

Both of us lost track of time and space, until the rabbi suddenly realized he had neglected his commitment. But I had convinced him – there was no doubt in my mind. He promised to help me. And I was happy. My soul had been drifting alone in the sea, almost drowning. I had thrown out a lifeline, but until now nobody had pulled me in. From this moment I knew that my soul would find peace. I knew I would become a Jew.

I followed Rabbi Michael out to the busy Helsinki street. Still standing on the sidewalk, before stepping into his car, Rabbi Michael took my head in his hands, gave me his blessing, and kissed me on the forehead. I will never forget that moment. Now I knew what action I had to take. I was on my way. My soul was being pulled to the shore, somebody had begun to care for it, had given it nourishment – in order that it should live.

I made sure that during every trip to the capital, I visited Rabbi Michael. Luckily, because of my different engagements, I had regular meetings in Helsinki, and my study schedule went smoothly. I have wonderful memories of these sessions with the rabbi. I always called to let him know in advance when we had trips coming up, in order to allow him to arrange his schedule. Once we were in Helsinki on a school trip at the museum when my phone rang. Rabbi Michael, in his spontaneous and often disorganized manner, was on the line. "Can you be at the synagogue in one hour – there will be a surprise for you." I looked at my students, grown up, but still in need of a leader. I turned to my colleague. "I have to go and meet a friend, you lead the rest of the tour for the day, and I will meet you later at our lodging." No problem! Full of curiosity, I walked determinedly towards the synagogue.

On the way I recalled his words. Did he mention something about a wedding? Approaching the Jewish quarter of Malmgatan, I saw crowds of beautifully-dressed people getting out of their cars. Many taxis and limousines seemed to be heading for the synagogue. I went inside to look for Rabbi Michael. I no longer felt as uncomfortable as I had during my first visit. Since then I had been to the synagogue a few times, sometimes with my wife, other times with the whole family. I always kept my *kippah* with me, the one Rabbi Michael gave me during my first visit. The time had come to put it on again.

There he was, in the crowd, talking to some of the visitors. I saw people I recognized from TV and parliament. It seemed to be a celebrity wedding, and all the Jews of Helsinki had gathered to celebrate. I did not belong there, nor was I a celebrity. But Rabbi Michael certainly treated me like one. "Now, my friend, you are going to see a Jewish wedding like you have never seen before." He was right, because this was the first Jewish wedding I had ever attended. The rabbi had promised a surprise, and he had certainly delivered on his promise. If it had not been for Rabbi Michael's warmth and consideration, I would have felt very much out of place, but since everybody saw I was his friend, they probably assumed I was some celebrity too – they just couldn't remember from where – so I mingled naturally in the crowd.

Later in the evening, I returned to the lodging where my students were staying, with a smile on my face and a secret in my heart. The secret of my first Jewish wedding. I couldn't wait to tell my family about it.

Spiritually uplifting events were rare occasions during the years when we were living without a formal religion. How wonderful then was the news of Dudu Fisher's visit to Sweden. We heard about the famous Israeli singer from Runa's brother Bill, who lives in Uppsala, where Dudu was going to perform. We drove 500 kilometers across Finland, and then embarked on a ten-hour voyage from Turku to Stockholm. It was well worth the effort. What an evening! All these songs about Yerushalayim…. The Yiddishe Mama…Adon Olam…and Dudu's rendition of Elvis's "It's Now or Never," emphasizing the urgent need for the Jewish people to return to *Eretz Yisrael*. When I hear these songs, even from a rusty street singer, tears well in my eyes. Hearing them at this concert, from the synagogue cantor who became a Broadway artist, in a packed concert hall crowded with 5,000 enthusiastic people, we felt as if we had been lifted to heaven. I believe God knew how lonely we were and how dry was our spiritual life. Just as early rains provide nourishment to the dry soil, so did this concert give life to our souls. It strengthened our desire for a Jewish life, a desire that had not yet been fulfilled, but was burning in our hearts. We would do whatever we could to ensure our connection to the people and the land.

The highlight for me of the whole conversion process was my Gilgal experience. No, I did not visit the biblical site near Jericho, but, I have my own connection to Gilgal. Just as the biblical Gilgal removed the disgrace of being slaves in Egypt, so did my *Brit Milah* (circumcision) do the same regarding my former church connection. After forty years in the desert, all the men who had not been circumcised on the way came under the knife of Joshua. "And after the whole nation had been circumcised they remained in the camp until they were healed. Then the Lord said to Joshua: 'This day have I rolled away the reproach of *Mitzrayim* (Egypt) from off you.'" (Joshua 5:8–9). Or as another translation words it: "Today I have removed from you the disgrace of being slaves in Egypt."

My *Brit Milah* had a similar meaning: it was a sign of my entrance into the Covenant of Abraham. But even more significant and concrete for me was how my circumcision served as a symbol of removing my past connection to a false church. Before a connection there is a separation; first exodus, then ingathering. I had to leave my former attachment before I could connect to a new one. It all seemed to come together in the ritual act of circumcision, dating back to the moment when God commanded Abraham to make the first cut instituting this Covenant. A cut connecting one person and one nation to Himself, carrying promises of blessings to the whole world. This was my moment to be connected to the Covenant, to become a carrier of the obligations, but also of the blessings.

I was overcome with an enormous sense of blessed privilege. How could this be happening to me? I was not worthy of it. But I had heard my master calling, and I was eager to answer. So it was with my conversion, beginning with the first critical questions about the Church, culminating in my *Brit Milah*. Now I had passed the point of no return. I had given my definite "yes" to the calling. After studying for about a year, we had reached the point of being welcomed into our new faith. Still it was regarded as a short study period. And truly it was all so new to us. I remember the first book Rabbi Michael gave me: *Sefer HaHinnuch*, the book of *mitzvah* (commandments) education. I read and read it over and over, but I have to admit that it raised more questions than it provided answers. I was confronted with a multitude of questions about how to put into practice all of God's commandments. In order to live a fully Jewish life you need to practice. The practical side of Judaism needs to be repeated and learned by imitating a teacher or a parent. This part of our education was missing since we lived so far away from any Jewish community. What we learned we started to practice to the best of our ability.

At our farewell party in Australia, years earlier, my wife had spoken about the biblical Ruth, not knowing how much of her own life would be a reflection of Ruth's. Now, our family was gathered in the home of the Helsinki rabbi, preparing for our immersion in the *mikvah* (ritual bath). And Ruth's story once more came to life.

We were choosing our Hebrew names. Rabbi Michael suggested my wife Runa take Ruth as her Hebrew name. To me he gave the name Shlomo, and I found no reason to object. Our daughters are Linda, who became Leah; Sara, who received the second name Rivka; Karolin, who became Yardena; and Josefin, who received the name Yudith.

Our naming process coincided with the time of Shavuot, when the Book of Ruth is read in synagogue. Ruth said to her mother-in-law Naomi: "Where you go, I will go and where you stay I will stay. Your people will be my people and your God my God." When Naomi realized that Ruth was determined to go with her, she stopped trying to convince her otherwise, while the story ends differently for Ruth's sister-in-law Orpa. Orpa also kept persisting that she wanted to go with Naomi to Eretz Yisrael, but shortly after we find her kissing Naomi good-bye, as she prepares to return to "her people and her gods." Action speaks louder than words, and Judaism is a very practical religion in which beliefs are strengthened and affirmed through practice.

Throughout the long process, my wife and I were in harmony along every step of the way – in our decision to leave the Church, convert, and finally make *aliyah* – growing together step by step. We never disagreed about our decisions, however far-reaching they were. We never thought of going back; we always cast our eyes forward, searching deeper into the Torah to fulfill the longing of our souls.

After my *Brit Milah*, it was time for us all to immerse in the *mikvah*. At the gathering afterwards in the Helsinki synagogue, the rabbi announced: "Now you are full members of the House of Israel." Those melodic words still ring like sweet music in my ears, "a full member of the House of Israel." He specifically pointed out the prohibition of doubting the authenticity of the conversion. What's done is done. There were no first- or second-class Jews. Rather, the opposite is the case: there are obligations in the Torah to be especially hospitable towards converts, "because you yourselves were once strangers in a strange land."

We were no longer "strangers," but we were like newborn babies, learning new practices and skills, learning to live. This process will take a lifetime and is never complete. Growing and learning, studying Torah, practicing the *mitzvot* are all ongoing tasks. This is the path we had taken. It felt so fulfilling, knowing our future direction, knowing who we were. Now I could believe I had a Jewish soul, and I had to learn to know my soul, to give it nourishment. I was still wondering about the great mystery of how God gives souls; what is the soul exactly, when do we get it, and is it possible that we can receive a new one? For now, I left those issues aside and was happy to enjoy the statement that was still ringing happily in my ears, when the rabbi declared us members of the House of Israel.

I again looked at my old coin. To my joy the engraving was becoming clearer. I could see whose coinage it was.

ELEVEN

A Land Flowing With Milk and Honey

ON A PARALLEL track with our conversion, we had also contacted the Jewish Agency and their representative in Helsinki, in preparation for our *aliyah*. The "*shaliach*" (a Jewish Agency representative who guides new immigrants in their *aliyah* process), Buki, was very helpful. Not wanting us to be under any false illusions, she candidly briefed us about the process of *aliyah* and integration into Israeli way of life: "First you will have one year of hell, then it will be paradise." Paradise or hell, whatever was in store for us, we were not moving to Israel to improve our lifestyle – we simply wanted to be here. If our goal had been to raise our standard of living, Finland or Australia would have been far more suitable choices. "But you have to be able to live. There are practical sides of life as well; you cannot support your family on an idealistic dream," Buki said. Coming to Israel means that many dreams will crash. If one is able to pick himself up after he has salvaged some of the pieces of his shattered dreams, then his *aliyah* will be a success. Buki suggested that we go on a pilot tour to find out for ourselves the different alternatives for our family. A visit might put our dreams in another perspective as well.

During this time of planning and dreaming, we also established contact with the British Olim Society in Israel, which deals with new immigrants from Britain but also from Scandinavia. I explained our situation, and they were very helpful in giving advice. The closer we came, however, to the completion of our conversion and our planned *aliyah*, the more wary the British Olim Society became in their encouragement. They were doubtful about our chances of surviving in Israel as new immigrants.

I felt tremendously saddened. On the one hand, I knew our *aliyah* would be difficult, so I could not blame the counsellors at the Society for their restraint. On the other hand, I knew that nothing could stop us from taking this step, so I would have appreciated some enthusiasm from their side. Why not be on fire for the sake of *aliyah*, in assisting Jews who are coming to the Promised Land? I did not let them discourage me. Instead I took the advice about a pilot tour and went to find out for myself.

I would have liked to have my wife with me for on-site consultations, but I was embarking on a reconnaissance tour by myself, making decisions for the whole family. I am hardly even trusted to go food shopping – always returning with the wrong items – and here I was "shopping" for my entire family's future! Based on my observations on this tour, we would be making decisions on where to settle, and hopefully I would be returning with good news about employment and schools.

I was overjoyed when I fastened my seat belt on an El Al flight from Helsinki to Tel Aviv on a beautiful August morning. That same afternoon I was to land in Israel, arriving as a Jew to look for a home for my family. How could something so new and strange be at the same time so familiar and so dear? I was going away, but I felt a strong sense of going home. Had I lived here before? For how long had my soul been uprooted from Jewish ground? I had time to ponder these questions again. Kabbalah talks about reincarnation, which could possibly explain our strange connection to everything Jewish.

The plane touched down; I was in *Eretz Yisrael* – in August, meaning it was extremely hot. I took a taxi to Tel Aviv where I looked up a hostel; my budget did not allow me to stay in a hotel. The hostel did not excite me, but never mind, it was Israel. I stayed up late, sitting on the balcony, taking in the hot, humid Middle Eastern summer air. In the morning I set out for the British Olim Society, where I had my first appointment. "So, how is your Hebrew?" "Well, after fourteen hours in Israel, we'd better talk English." After just a few hours in the country, a lack of Hebrew is acceptable. But what if the same question hits you years later? The holy tongue is a difficult language to learn, and this is one of the many tough realities of *aliyah*.

"We suggest you visit the Absorption Centers in Nazareth and Ra'anana," was the advice I received. We were too old to be accepted into a kibbutz; families with small children are suited to kibbutz life, not families with teenagers. To start out on our own was unthinkable, as we had virtually no financial assets. An Absorption Center, a "*Merkaz Klita*," seemed to be the most viable option. I left the British Olim Society offices a few hours later with appointments pencilled in my diary for the next few days. I seemed to be off to a good start and with hope in my heart, I clutched onto a thick folder filled with information and contacts.

Sitting in the bus heading north, we passed some Arab villages, then crossed the beautiful Jezreel Valley, and continued up the winding road to Nazareth. I was constantly asking myself: "Can I picture my family here? How much am I really asking of them?" Suddenly I was glad I had come on the pilot tour by myself, envisaging what might have been the outcome if the family had come along.

It did not take me long to realize that Nazareth was the wrong place for us. Driving through the town, so familiar to me from the Christian holy books, I noticed a sign in a window that read: "Merry Christmas." In the window of a butcher's shop, I saw an ad for "pork meat" and another sign pointed the way to "the Church of Jesus Christ." I was shocked. It was for this reason we wanted to leave Finland – the holidays, the food, the Church.

It was a shame, because the *Merkaz Klita* in Upper Nazareth was quite new and beautifully located on a hillside with magnificent views. The staff were friendly and helpful, making my decision all the more difficult. I turned to my next appointment in my diary, the *Merkaz Klita* in Ra'anana.

What a relief! Ra'anana seemed like the perfect place for us. Here, I could picture my daughters making friends, socializing. It was a beautiful, picturesque town – but what about the *Merkaz Klita*? Will it meet the same standard? Walking to the Absorption Center, I thought about my family, and how spoiled we were when it came to our creature comforts. And what if this was our last option, and it was not acceptable? We had no choice. We would have to move here anyway. I just had to think of a reasonable explanation, and hope that the girls would understand.

There it was, a large complex of buildings that seemed to fulfill what its name suggested: it absorbed a lot of people. But that did not scare me. The atmosphere was warm. Already in the lobby I met some friendly newcomers who greeted me as if I was going to become part of the family.

The housemother, Zippi, showed me around and let me take a look at one of the apartments. As a family of six, we would qualify for a three-room apartment, which meant two bedrooms, and a small living space, including a tiny kitchen equipped with a fridge and two gas burners. It was nothing special, but considering the lack of alternatives, it was acceptable – for me. The challenge now was to explain to the rest of the family how we would be living for our first year in Israel. I thought my detailed illustration of the place was spot on, until the girls saw it when we moved in three months later. I was inspired by Joshua and Caleb when I reported back my findings to my family. Nothing could be done to change what I had seen, but I could select which information to share, emphasizing the positive, while omitting the negative.

I wanted to give a good report from the Land, like Joshua and Caleb on their first spy mission into Israel some 3,500 years earlier. The ten other spies saw that the Canaanites living in the Land were very strong, and they reported their findings back to the people, with terrible consequences. "We will die," they said and they sure did. The entire generation was to die during their forty years in the desert. One year for each day the spies had been on their mission. Not so for Joshua and Caleb. They were the only ones of their generation who were granted entry into *Eretz Yisrael*.

It is a truism that we tend to get what we expect, from both a positive and negative perspective. Therefore it is important to be careful with our thoughts and words, and to concentrate on creativity rather than destruction. The ten negative spies saw the powerful nations inside the Land, the battles they were going to lose. And lo and behold, they lost. The two spies with a positive attitude, Joshua and Caleb, saw the same land, inhabited by the same strong people, but they did not verbalize the negative aspects. Joshua and Caleb drew strength from their faith in God who had promised to give the Land to them. The inhabitants might be strong, they said, but it does not matter because we are stronger.

"The land we passed through and explored is exceedingly good. If the Lord is pleased with us, He will lead us into that land, a land flowing with milk and honey, and will give it to us. Only do not rebel against the Lord. And do not be afraid of the people of the land because we will swallow them up. Their protection is gone, but the Lord is with us. Do not be afraid of them" (Numbers 14:8).

On my pilot tour, the attitude of some of the advisers I encountered left me feeling sad and disappointed. I came to Israel to receive encouragement and inspiration for the move, which I knew would be very difficult for our family. I was well aware of our lack of financial assets, lack of Hebrew, and lack of suitable professions. Could it get any worse? Not really. Were there any other examples of people who were less suitable for *aliyah* than us? No. But I did not want to be told what I already knew. I was going to go through with it anyway. What I needed was moral support and encouragement.

My next step was to go to the Jewish Agency in Jerusalem. Without their blessing, I was told I would not make it. There are many capital cities in the world, but there is only one Jerusalem. How different and holy was Jerusalem! I was surrounded by this feeling as soon as I got off the bus on Jaffa Road. I was not used to wearing a *kippah* (traditional Jewish head covering for men). I had been a Jew only for a few months, but in this holy city, I felt I had to cover my head and in an instant, the *kippah* was in place.

Before doing anything else, I headed to the *Kotel* (the Western Wall), the remnant of the Second Temple and the closest Jews can come to the place chosen by God to manifest His glory on earth. The place every Jew faces in prayer wherever in the world he might be. I caressed the huge, old stones, so smooth from all the hands that touched them. I felt a connection to the generations who had stood there praying to the One God, whose glory once rested on this place at the inauguration of the Temple (II Chron. 7). This was not just an archeological site. It was a holy place chosen by God, in which His Name will dwell forever. In the coming days this will also be the site for the third Temple, the eternal one. "My eyes and my heart will always be there," says God in His response to Solomon's prayer (II Chron. 7:16).

The past is great, but the future is even greater. God removes his presence (temporarily) from places, but not from His people. In *Haftarat Tetzaveh* (the prophet text read on the Shabbat when the Torah portion *Tetzaveh* is recited) we are reminded through the prophet Ezekiel how God withdrew his *Shechinah* (divine glory) from the Temple because of the sins of the people, leaving it an empty shell vulnerable to the Babylonian Army. The strong message is that God will nevertheless share the exile with the people and bring them home again. Ezekiel also had a clear vision of the third Temple being erected and God's presence returning: "When the Lord brought back the captives to Zion, we were like men who dreamed. Our mouths were filled with laughter, our tongues with songs of joy. Then it was said among the nations, 'The Lord has done great things for them.' The

Lord has done great things for us, and we are filled with joy. Restore our fortunes, O Lord, like streams in the Negev. Those who sow in tears will reap with songs of joy. He who goes out weeping carrying seed to sow, will return with songs of joy, carrying sheaves with him." (Psalm 126).

My moment of prayer at the Wall filled me with strength, which I needed for my next visit, this time to the Jewish Agency. Little did I know how much strength and courage I would actually need for this appointment. The meeting seemed to be well prepared. My file was already open when I entered the office. The information they had about me and my family was quite detailed, but in their view it left room for many questions. Their biggest concern was my education; coming to Israel with a theological degree from a Christian University was not a promise for a great future. Suddenly I understood their suspicions. Was there some organization backing us and taking care of us from the day we were to set foot in Israel? I had to use all my powers of persuasion to reassure them that this was not the case. We had no hidden agendas. We were for real. We were Jews. No country in the world could replace Israel for us. Making *aliyah* meant coming home and beginning a new life.

The Jewish Agency official was still doubtful about our chances of success. I agreed it would be difficult, but continued to explain our case, because I saw she was beginning to listen. "It is neither logical nor rational for us to come, but as a Jew I need and want to live within the borders of *Eretz Yisrael*. If I were to act only according to rationale, I would not come, but that is not how I have arrived at this decision. This is a decision we have taken in faith. This is my answer to God's promise of a Land for His people, a land not only with a great history, but a land with an even greater future. If I'm not coming home I'm disappointing He who prepared all this for me. I have to listen to my heart, to my soul. You can have only one loyalty. You cannot serve two masters. Compromise makes you weak, it divides your strength. I have made radical moves in my life, but I still have strength for one more move – to Israel. My loyalty is with the God of Israel, with His people and His Land. Now I am a Jew. If I'm not coming home to Israel, who is…?"

I could have kept going, but I restrained myself. It seemed to me that the official was moved and I did not want to stir up any difficult feelings. She wiped tears from her eyes. "I'm thinking of my own family back home in the States; I only wish that they were as strongly Zionist as you are, and would come on *aliyah*. I'm the only one here out of my family, and I'm always trying to encourage them to come, but so far with no luck. I hope that they one day will talk like you and make the same decision."

I had made my point very clear. It was obvious we would receive our recommendation for *aliyah*. And their suspicion? For the moment, it seemed they had put it aside, but they would be checking up on me later.

So far, I had found an acceptable place to live, and had succeeded in convincing the Jewish Agency of our suitability for *aliyah*. These achievements made me feel that my pilot trip was going well. But there was still a major challenge ahead – looking for a job. Through the British Olim Society and the Jewish Agency, I received a few contacts, but they did not lead to anything concrete. To get a job, either you need to be sent to Israel by the company you work for abroad, or you need to be permanently living in the country. Neither of these alternatives were relevant to us yet, so it seemed that I would have to wait until we were permanent residents in the country before I could begin job searching.

After one hot, hectic week in Israel, I was on my way back to Finland. As we flew over the beautiful Mediterranean, I felt happy and convinced that the family would be on its way very soon. After all, we were on the waiting list to the *Merkaz Klita* in Ra'anana, and as soon as they had room for us, we could move as soon as we wanted. I had a feeling that our daughters would like what they saw from the pictures of my trip – the decision which pictures to show them was mine.

TWELVE

Our Personal Exodus

In NOVEMBER 1996, after all our belongings were packed in a container, we were ready to leave. Our long-awaited journey had begun, only three months after my pilot tour. We took the train from Kokkola to Helsinki. Saying our good-byes to our family at the train station was an emotionally charged affair. My sister came to say good-bye, as did some of my wife's relatives. For the girls it was particularly difficult. They had left some very dear friends behind, and did not know when they would see them again.

As for me, this could be my last time in Finland. I had no desire to go back, nor any reason. It was as if I were leaving Egypt, my own private exodus. To me, Finland represents Christianity, another outlook, other priorities and loyalties. My focus had shifted radically.

The train started to move. My hometown faded away in the distance. When our eyes left the window, we sat down and faced forward, and realized that we were now facing our new homeland. Suddenly we felt an enormous sense of joy and fulfillment that we were finally on our way. After all, we had endured many hardships to arrive at this point, and we did not know what was to come. Sitting in the train with my family, all of us together, embarking upon a new destiny, brought so many feelings to the surface. I was grateful to God that this day had arrived. I had the same feelings of gratitude towards my family – imagine having them all there with me! If I could just protect them until I see them settled in the Land of Israel, see them rooted in yet another place, hopefully this time for good. And I prayed that God would take good care of us, because the journey we had now embarked upon was a difficult one. We thought we knew what we were doing, but how could we really know? Despite our strong faith we were taking a leap into an unknown future. Every challenge from now on, no matter how big or small, might turn the agony towards me: "Dad, why did we do this, take us back." I was terrified by this thought and I prayed even more intensely. During our long journey into the unknown, many questions would arise, maybe a desire to go back, or a longing for something of the old country. To my daughters' credit, I must admit that they have never once blamed me, despite many hardships that would have made me understand if they had chosen to.

Sitting there in the train cabin, with the family so close together, some memories came to me. Only with God's protection and providence were we all there. It could have been so different. During the winter preceding our *aliyah*, the girls had gone into town on a cold and icy day. The oldest had just received her driver's license, so the girls were enjoying their freedom. On the way home, the car went into a spin on the slippery road, and overturned in a deep ditch. Miraculously the girls escaped unhurt. Shocked and frightened they crawled out through the broken windows. Their lives were saved, thank God! That was the only thing that mattered. We paid little attention to the fact that the car was a write-off and was sold for scrap metal.

Soon after, during the same winter, my wife and one of our daughters put their guardian angels to the test once again. During blizzard conditions in busy morning traffic – Finns go to work even if it's snowing heavily – the same event repeated itself. Despite the slow pace and careful driving, the car turned around and passed into the opposite lane, where heavy timber trucks are usually on their way to the saw mill. Gliding like a stone on ice, the car came to a halt undamaged, two inches from a power pole on the opposite side of the road. What about the passengers? Shocked but not hurt, they continued on the icy road to work.

Considering that we had never had any accidents before, although we had been driving in winter conditions for many years, these events seemed a bit unusual. And that was not all. My wife experienced yet another accident that winter with the same lucky escape. What about me? Was I free from similar incidents? Two weeks before we were to set out on the train, taking us away from our old life, it was my turn. I was on my last business trip in my capacity as headmaster. I was alone in the car on a one-hour drive to a meeting with other school principals. The morning was foggy, but this was not unusual, and the traffic flowed normally. I reached a section where there was a moose warning, a normal sight on Finnish roads, where these big creatures often cross – or is it we humans who are crossing their paths? In Australia we got used to seeing similar signs that warned about kangaroos jumping across the road. Without much coordination, the paths of the animals and humans sometimes cross with fatal results.

Suddenly, without any time to react, I saw something approaching from the right. In a twinkling of an eye my mind had just enough time to process the data: "a big head with big horns." Yet there was no time for precautions. I felt a heavy bounce, as the huge creature landed on my engine hood and was thrown by the impact. I managed to stop the car at the side of the road and call the police, for insurance purposes and to take care of the animal. I was unharmed. I did not care much about the meeting after this accident. I was happy to have escaped unhurt from my first close encounter with the king of the Finnish forest.

The train shook as it approached a station on the way southwards. I felt as if I were waking up from a bad dream when I realized that these were real memories that were passing through my mind.

"The Finnish November landscape is quickly passing by the train window. The snow has fallen and partly melted again. It is wet and cold. Everything looks like a black and white photo, no joyful colors, only brown, gray and some white. Finland is truly sparsely populated, with great distances between cities. The journey is to the capital, and for every kilometer southwards my joy is increasing. Finland belongs to the past. I'm leaving everything that Finland stands for – a Christianity that was always on the wrong track. I'm leaving my Egypt, where my song died and my soul longed to be away. I'm leaving the cold." My wife wrote her comments while the train sped along, carrying us closer to realizing our dream.

We had to wait one more day until we would experience the warm Israeli air. Arriving in Helsinki, we spent the last night at a hotel in preparation for going to the Israeli Embassy in the morning, before heading to the airport. The Embassy was a familiar place by now. We had visited there many times, but this time was different – now we were coming to get our entry visas as permanent residents, not as tourists. The Embassy personnel were extremely friendly, especially one young man, dressed immaculately in a black suit, white shirt, and black tie. He seemed to have nothing better to do than challenge our crazy decision. "You won't be able to take it, the culture is too different – take it from me, in one month you will be on a flight back." The way he talked was typically Israeli. Everything is everybody's business. Like a brother he was sharing his opinion and dispensing advice. The girls were flattered. He looked like a James Bond type, and maybe he was one. I tried to work out what his hidden agenda might be. It certainly seemed as if there was one. And it was professional, not personal.

He promised to visit us soon to see how we were coping. Believe it or not, two weeks later somebody knocked on the door at the *Merkaz Klita*. It was Yoram, the young man from the Embassy. I hardly recognized him. This time he was casually dressed and looked even younger. He told me he had a business meeting in the neighborhood and took the opportunity to drop in. "You are doing a great job," I thought to myself. I could not help but connect his behavior and visit to the suspicions of the Jewish Agency. It did not matter to me. If they wanted to check up on me, that was fine. He could see that we had told the truth. We lived in a small flat in the Absorption Center trying to stretch every shekel to pay for food. Certainly there was no missionary organization secretly supporting us.

We received the necessary documents from the Embassy, and went to our hotel to spend our last night in Finland. The girls were obviously nervous about their new homeland, which they had never seen, and were especially curious about the conditions of our first home in Israel, asking me again and again to describe the apartment at the *Merkaz Klita*, comparing it to the hotel. "Does it look like this?" they asked, with a tone that indicated their true meaning: "Is it as bad as this?" This was not a five-star hotel, rather a hostel-type accommodation, not as fancy as the hotels they remembered from our trips to and from Australia in places such as Hawaii, Toronto, Singapore, and Tokyo. Without entering into detail, I told them it was the same standard, leaving them feeling curious until they could judge for themselves the following day.

The check-in at Helsinki airport took hours. Security did not leave anything to chance. Most of our ample luggage had stayed at the train station overnight. Because it was already marked with the destination ISRAEL on every package, every box and suitcase had to be opened for security reasons. At the check-in, we caught our first glimpse of other new immigrants. These were Jews from Russia, making *aliyah* via Finland, boarding the same flight.

A pleasant, warm November air enveloped us welcomingly when we stepped out of the airplane at Ben-Gurion airport. At last we could feel Israeli soil under our feet. The immigration procedure, including issuing our immigration passport, the *"Teudat Oleh,"* was over in less than an hour. We were ready to make our way to the *Merkaz Klita*. We were driven in a large taxi, overloaded with all the belongings that were supposed to be adequate for about a year. The rest of our goods were to be shipped to Israel when we had rented our own apartment. It was nighttime, but the Absorption Center seemed to be very much alive.

Before we had even finished unloading the taxi, a handful of young boys were offering to help. Maybe four blond girls caught their attention more than the heavy boxes, yet suddenly the luggage did not seem heavy at all. Whatever the motive, the help was appreciated. Without it we would have been running up and down the stairs until morning.

Now it was my turn to be nervous. My moment of truth was arriving. I had already seen the apartment, described it, and shown my beautiful pictures of the exotic courtyard with its flourishing trees. Now it was my family's turn for first impressions.

The girls ran upstairs, rushed into the apartment, eagerly checking it out room by room. When they realized there were no more rooms – only two bedrooms for six people – they slowed down, looked around, checked the bathroom once again, and the tiny kitchen. I saw disappointment in their faces. "Dad," they said with one voice. Teenagers don't always agree, but now they were unanimous, and they seemed to be united against me. "Dad, this is not the place you described to us. Are we going to stay here?"

"Yes, this is it, we are going to stay here." There was no sudden outburst of anger. The girls just needed some time to collect themselves; some private time to "mourn" their home in Finland, their clean, spacious rooms, their own belongings. They sat down on the beds, quietly shedding some tears. My wife and I began to tidy up; we wanted to show them that we could make this small space our cozy, little home, our own hideaway from which to make a new beginning.

It worked. When the girls saw the apartment filled with our belongings, smiles emerged from behind the tears. They were inspired to start decorating their rooms. Sara took the lead – out of all our daughters, she is the home decorator. Whenever we moved, she was the first to set up her room, to the envy of the other sisters. "This is not fair, your room is so cute," they would say to Sara. Then she would help them decorate their rooms as well. This time there was not so much room for decorating. The girls shared the bedrooms, two to a room, while my wife and I had the living room all to ourselves. It was late at night, or rather, early morning. The girls had already unpacked their bags, hung some pictures on the walls, and suddenly the place looked like a home. When we hugged each other after all the effort and strain of this first night at the *Merkaz Klita*, we knew that we could make it.

My worries had always centered around the girls, not to mention Ruth's reaction – she is after all an interior designer and very close to being a perfectionist. How would she take it? It was also hard for her, but on the other hand, her determination and sense of Zionism were strong. That's why I did not worry as much about her adjustment. The tears we shed did not dim our vision, rather they made us see clearer, and further, beyond the immediate reality to a distant yet beautiful future.

"Tea is served," Ruth called from the kitchen. She did not need to shout since we were all close by. We enjoyed a well-deserved evening snack in the midst of all the action and emotion. The welcoming package, consisting of some tea, coffee, and biscuits, which the housemother placed on the kitchen table, did wonders. We all felt better. Life had started at *Merkaz Klita*.

It took me a while to fall asleep that night. Lying down I could see out through the window. I saw the stars in the sky. I remembered Abraham and the promise God made to him when He said to him: "Look at the stars, if you are able to number them, so shall your seed be…unto thy seed have I given this land" (Genesis 15:5, 18). We were now under the same heaven open to Abraham, in the land promised to him and his seed. It was amazing that *we* were able to count ourselves among the seed of Abraham, that we were actually in the Promised Land. It was a wish come true. But it was so much more. It was a biblical promise being fulfilled and we were part of it. Our prayers were answered. How privileged and grateful I felt.

THIRTEEN

A Taste of Israeli Culture

THE FOLLOWING MORNING we explored Ra'anana together. The girls tasted their first Israeli falafel, which they enjoyed, to my enormous relief. Every time we experienced something new, which happened quite frequently, Ruth and I registered our daughters' reaction. Every approval was like an investment in our trust account, and we didn't deposit the disapprovals. The "honeymoon" of making *aliyah* lasted for a few days. Soon Sara, Karolin, and Josefin had to begin school while Linda started Hebrew lessons together with myself and Ruth. We were surprised and delighted when Shoshana and Nehemya, friends of our friends in Finland, called to invite us to Jerusalem for our first Shabbat in Israel. To us, this signified a blessed beginning.

It was "story time" in the ulpan class, where we were to learn Hebrew. Learning Hebrew all day long was difficult and every now and then, we needed to break the monotony. One of the students asked if he could tell the class a story that illustrated what it means to make *aliyah*.

A man had a dream that an angel came to him and granted him a request allowing him a peek into the coming world. There are two options, either heaven or hell. You may look into the two options to see which one might appeal to you more, which alternative to choose when you die. "Fine," the man thought, "First I want to take a look at what heaven is like."

His request was granted. He saw green fields, and friendly people walking around peacefully enjoying the beautiful scenery. "Nice, but let's take a look at the other alternative," the man asked. God granted him a visit into hell. What did he see? Hell was a crowded place. Noisy, loud, with people smoking, but more his style, he had to admit. It seemed more appealing after all. So he told God he'd rather choose hell when he dies. Eventually the man died and his request was fulfilled. He was introduced to hell.

This time it was different. It was too loud, people were too rude. There was so much smoke and fire, it was dangerous and scary. The man turned back and told his escorting angel his regrets: "This is not what I saw before." The angel told the man: "Yes, it is exactly the same place, the difference is: then you were a tourist, now you are an *Oleh Hadash* (new immigrant)."

Although we hadn't been here long, we felt we could relate to this story. There is an enormous difference between coming to Israel as a tourist, for a week, when everybody treats you in a friendly manner, and making *aliyah*, when you become a full-fledged Israeli, without special treatment. Getting established in Israel means going through all the bureaucracy needed for living. This substantial amount of paperwork must be completed in a relatively short period of time. What you did in your old country over many years must be done in this new country in a few days or weeks. Go to the Interior Ministry to receive your ID; run errands to the immigration department; open a bank account; register for health insurance; get a phone line, a gas connection, an electricity account. There is no end to it. Converting your driver's license alone will take you to five different places, plus some driving lessons and a test drive. Bearing in mind that you can only visit a maximum of one place per day, these kinds of procedures will keep you busy for quite a while.

But why can you only visit one place a day? Why does it have to take so long? I began with an optimistic attitude. I set myself a schedule to visit two departments in the morning and two in the afternoon. I did not even manage to finish the first one. It was on strike! I took a bus to get there early, still arriving hours later than I expected because of the heavy traffic, only to find a note on the door announcing a strike for that day.

I learned the hard way that nothing is done on the first visit. Even if you find out the opening hours beforehand, you will most likely turn up during the wrong hours. When you finally do get inside, and have sat out the waiting period, you will most likely be missing some crucial documents, and have to return another day with all the necessary papers. But be careful, because the opening hours for the following day are probably different.

It takes a lot of patience to make *aliyah*. "*Savlanut*" is a Hebrew word you learn quickly because without patience, you won't make it.

It is important, though, to be fair to your new country and to yourself. When did you ever before have to do all this in such a limited period of time? What system in your old country could handle thousands of new immigrants any more smoothly? Language barriers between newcomers and officials doesn't make it any easier. Still, most of the people you deal with speak either English or Russian, so there is a choice. The people who try to push in front of you on line, or who are impolite, are also the first ones to help you if you need assistance or translation. In Israel, we are one big family, for better and for worse.

Sitting in a crowded waiting room gives you time to study your fellow immigrants and reflect on our common stories. When you see people from different continents, cultures, and languages, they might seem so different to you. We are all here, though, with a common goal: to settle the land and fulfill the promise that was made to our forefathers. This perspective helps you be patient. Don't rush! You have come this far, after waiting for a thousand years, to be part of the fulfillment of prophecies – you can easily take your time in the line.

Driving in Israel is an experience in itself. Everybody knows their rights, or what they think are their rights, and they're eager to demonstrate them to you. Body language, gestures, beeping the horn, shouting out the window: these signs are loud enough to make the message absolutely clear. When I would wait at a red light, I wondered what technical device Israelis had connected to their cars, because the second the light changed to yellow, they were already honking the horn impatiently. For a long time, I was absolutely certain that there was a sensor installed in most cars. It turned out that the sensor was sitting at the steering wheel, eager to let you know that it's time to go.

You might feel that you are in the midst of enemies, but you are wrong. If you have a flat tire or engine problems, you need only wait seconds before someone stops to help. In Israel, you stand up for your brother when he needs you.

We laugh at the joke about the new immigrant, because we see ourselves in him. There is a difference between being in Israel as a tourist and settling here. No doubt about it. The real, and the most important, difference is that making *aliyah* means you are coming home to live among family. As one Ukrainian immigrant told me, "In the Ukraine I had fears; here I feel welcomed, I have a home where I belong."

Making *aliyah* impacts on every aspect of life. Work and education, finances, and friends. Add to this a conversion and your difficulties
increase. It's impossible to know how long integration into a new country,
nationality, religion, society, profession, and language really takes. Such a
multitude of changes can't happen overnight. Yet this is the challenge my
family and I chose – of our own free will. Could we realistically expect it to
be easy, or even possible? I believe that my daughters will recognize when
their integration is complete. As for me, I believe my integration depends
on my own will, but practically speaking, it will never be complete – not
during my lifetime.

What is integration? When are you absorbed into a society? Full
command of Hebrew, applying for a job with a degree from the Hebrew
University, being confident in halachic issues; all these things might take
me the rest of my life. But if I compare my attitude to that of my Israeli
brother who dislikes Israel and would rather live somewhere else, then I
already feel more integrated than he. I love this Land and have dedicated
the rest of my life to Israel. I'm on board and the ship is sailing. I have time
to learn what it takes.

But how much time? A year, or two, or five maybe? No, rather a
lifetime. There are aspects of living in Israel in which you will never feel
completely connected. On the other hand, it is up to you to set the time
frame for your integration. It is up to you to keep on fighting, to continue
working towards your dream. It is up to you to set the model for your
children. After ten months at the *Merkaz Klita*, working as a cleaner to
make a living, I hadn't yet reached the happy moment when I could celebrate and shout: "We made it!" Unfortunately, during this critical time,
some immigrants leave. But don't look back! Remember the sea that split,
it closed up again. Why? To destroy the Egyptian Army, who drowned
in the closing waters. And also to say: this is a one-way road; there is no
reason to use it again. And Lot's family leaving Sodom were commanded
not to look back.

I am not judgmental of those who for so many different personal
reasons find it impossible to stay here. I am talking only about our case.
We left our Egypt – a Christian life in a Christian country. Getting out
meant staying out.

In our new country, did the manna fall and the quails land on our
table? No. In *Eretz Yisrael*, one must labor in order to earn a living. In fact

there are quails for sale in the supermarkets, but to have the money to buy them, you need to do something other than study in ulpan class. The first five months of our stay at the *Merkaz Klita*, during which time a new immigrant still receives some monetary support from the state, we studied Hebrew in the class provided. In hindsight, this time seemed worry-free. Going to class every morning, doing homework in the afternoon. Living simply in order to stay within our budget. The closer we came to the end of our maximum one-year stay at the center, the more we began to feel the reality of our new life. We needed jobs, and an apartment in which to live.

In Israel everything seems to happen through contacts. But it takes time to create a social network. Luckily there were people who had been through this already, who understood the situation and were ready to help. Max Grunberg, from Holland, had also lived in the *Merkaz Klita* a few years earlier with his family. I met him at the Shabbat services in the *Merkaz Klita* Synagogue. The Jewish Outreach Center, headed by Rabbi S. Weiss, organized these services. Here I adapted to the beautiful practice of wearing the *tallit* (prayer shawl) during the *Shacharit* morning service, and learnt the importance of donning *tefillin* (phylacteries) every weekday morning. This *Beit Knesset* (synagogue) was the first that I had attended on a regular basis, and it was an extremely important part of my life, both for prayer and for building a social network.

Max helped me find my first real job in Israel. He knew somebody who was looking for workers to pack first-aid kits. I could spare a few hours here and there for this job, as long as it gave me a few extra shekels. The story about "somebody who knows somebody who might need somebody" is famous, simply because it is the best employment agency on the market. This is true especially in my case, but also for many other new immigrants who have to start their careers in Israel from a very humble point. I had not yet mastered the language and my degree in theology was practically worthless. I could not afford to be fussy when it came to accepting a job, because I did not even know what I was looking for. When people asked me what I wanted to do, I could not answer them. I knew my strengths, but they revolved around people, and before I could put my skills to use, I needed a language, preferably Hebrew.

The time to move out of the *Merkaz Klita* was approaching fast. Our first year in Israel had flown by. Our life in those two rooms, without a

TV and a lot of other items we had once regarded as essential, had been surprisingly smooth and trouble-free. Our three youngest daughters had begun school. Linda, the eldest, who graduated in Finland, joined myself and Ruth in the Hebrew ulpan class. It was a bizarre situation to sit in the same class with our own daughter. We were very proud of the competent way in which she learned the new language. But I don't think she was as proud of us oldies.

For the fourteen-year-old twins, Karolin and Josefin, we found a school nearby with special classes for new immigrants. It was difficult for them to catch up with all the subjects in a new language, and the girls were frustrated to see their grades drop when they were used to getting top grades back in Finland and Australia. The principal called us to the twins' school and, obviously, we wondered what the matter was. We met with him and the class teacher. We were pleased to hear that they were satisfied with the girls' progress, but they had one concern that they wanted to share with us. The teachers had witnessed some strange behavior from the boys in the school since the girls' arrival. They told us how the boys even climbed on the windows to get a glimpse of the blond Scandinavians in class. The teachers were slightly embarrassed by the boys' way of approaching the new students, so they wanted to tell us themselves rather than letting us hear it from our daughters.

One of the biggest advantages of the Absorption Center is the way it functions as a meeting place for young people. This was a key to our daughters' survival – indeed for all of us. Since the apartment was too small to spend much time inside, the girls would run downstairs, and always found friends to talk to. If we had moved straight into an apartment of our own, we would have been much more isolated.

Our daughter Sara, who was in her last year of school, received a placement in an English High School, a boarding school in a nearby town. She spent most weekdays at the school, but always returned home for Shabbat. The academic work was still very tough because this was the year of graduation exams, which she had to complete in Hebrew. She did graduate, which was an achievement in itself.

I continued to turn to Max in my search for a job that would provide me with an income that would support my family. He in turn engaged his friends, who talked to their friends. How can we find a job for this new immigrant from Finland? They took my dilemma seriously. This shows a wonderful side of *aliyah*. There are after all people who welcome you in the most caring way. At the time, our friends never said it, but now, looking back, I think that they were really worried. When it came to finding a job, I was a difficult case.

What about my dear wife? How was she doing all this time? She had her work in design, her education as a nurse, and restaurant experience. Later on, it was her cooking and baking skills that would become her career. Her creativity became known when she began to do some catering jobs from the tiny kitchen in the *Merkaz Klita*. There were two small gas burners and a little oven that she borrowed. It must have been the smallest catering kitchen ever, complete with a rabbi checking the *kashrut* (standards in Jewish dietary law, what is permitted and what is forbidden to eat). How wonderful it felt when people from the "network society" dropped by to place their orders, and happily picked up their ready-prepared Shabbat lasagne and carrot cake on Friday afternoon.

By the time we had to move out of the *Merkaz Klita*, I still did not have a permanent job. It was a scary time, because our rent was going to rise from 600 subsidized shekels to 600 non-subsidized dollars. How did we even dare to look for a place? But what choice did we have? A realist might have suggested moving back to Finland, but the thought never crossed our minds. My wife certainly did not mention it and – to my relief – neither did our daughters.

For a while I was working as a construction worker at a small building company. I knew it would not last long, but I took the job out of necessity. I could not sign a rental contract while I was unemployed. Whatever the job, it was better than nothing. Our rental agent and a friend signed as guarantors. This happens in Israel, where people are looking for opportunities to do *mitzvot* – good deeds to help others. It was crazy, but it felt great. We found a very nice apartment, which even the girls liked.

Meanwhile I was not simply waiting for opportunities to drop down on me. I have a thick file of applications I submitted to different companies, responding to their advertisements, as well as direct applications to companies that interested me. I went to all the *aliyah* organizations, Scandinavian Embassies and companies, but I had no luck until one of Max's friends, Verner, called me. He had a friend who knew a Finn working for a company in the furniture industry. So was I experienced in this field? No! Did I have a technical education? No! Was I in great need of a job? Yes! Was I practical, willing to try anything? Yes! I was curious, and since I had nothing to lose I decided to meet my potential employers. It turned out to be the Steelcase dealer in Israel, an office environment company, seeking workers for its next big project to install open space workstations for Intel. Exactly one year to the day after landing in Israel I began working for Steelcase. To my surprise I am still employed there seven years later – not as an installer anymore, but as a project manager, leading projects from the first client contact to completion of hundreds of workstations, for Cellcom, Volkswagen, Citibank, Continental Airlines, and numerous other companies.

Here was an opportunity to learn a new profession. During my time as an installer, I got to know every screw and every panel of the different furniture systems. Combining this knowledge with my management experience and people skills, I still needed some AutoCAD training, and then I was ready to take on a new challenge. After learning Computer Aided Design I was able to do office planning on computer as part of my job.

Recently, on one of my business meetings in Tel Aviv, I happened to drive along Dizengoff Street, past the central plaza with its water cascade (by Yaacov Agam). Suddenly I was struck by a memory. On my pilot tour, prior to our *aliyah*, I had stayed in a nearby hostel. I remembered how I had sat on the park bench, looking at the water cascade, trying to figure out how to find employment and a place for the family to live. In hindsight, I realized that the pilot tour was useful, but it was impossible in such a short time to achieve what I had set out to do. Now, seven years later, I had finally achieved my goals. I was driving my own company car, conducting meetings with architects, planning the furniture systems for office buildings that touched the skies of Tel Aviv. On my pilot tour this new country had seemed so frightening to me. I knew nobody. I felt lost, as if I had dropped down from the sky into a strange world. Suddenly – as if waking from a dream – I seemed to have passed this point of memory and I realized that I have come a long way after all, despite the many difficult years in between. Silently, I thanked God for the temperament He gave me: I easily forget the hardships and seem to remember only the good things in life. Now, I had contacts, I knew people, and I knew where I was headed. Admiring the skyscrapers, I not only felt awe and admiration – I knew the people inside, I sold the chairs they are sitting on, and I planned the offices they are working in. I was a perfect example of somebody not suitable for *aliyah*.

I like to think that I have proven the nay-sayers wrong, all those who were hesitant about our chances for survival in this jungle.

I'm filled with gratitude towards God and man. To God, because He gave me faith, hope, persistence, and adaptability skills that are essential for my survival. And I am grateful to so many people I have met during these first hard years of *aliyah*. Because many of you were God's emissaries, without knowing it – giving me a chance, showing confidence in me, helping me along. My family is always on my mind, because this is a struggle we are facing together. We are fighters in the same unit. My wife is there all the time, providing support, comfort, and encouragement with her enthusiasm and love for Israel. And our lovely daughters who never give in to all the hardships, who are always trying to see the positive side, always doing their best, knowing that Israel is their future as well.

FOURTEEN

The Challenge of Conversion

WHAT IS MORE difficult – being a stranger among your own family, or being a stranger among strangers? During our last years in Finland, when we did not share the faith of our relatives, our contact with our extended family was more like a scratch on the surface, rather than a deep relationship. We could feel the roots slowly being pulled up. If a tree is pulled out by its roots, it will soon die if it is not planted again in time, in fertile soil, watered and nurtured.

Being a stranger among strangers, on the other hand, is a situation that can be worked on. But having alienated yourself from the faith of your family, you helplessly grow apart from them. It is unfortunate, but it is part of the process and the price of conversion. It is difficult to describe how we felt when we realized that there was no aspect of our lives that would remain unaffected by our conversion. Yet we were not forced to go through with it. We initiated every step ourselves. As we distanced ourselves from our family, we felt a sadness as the natural, close connection weakened. Still it was not very painful because the connection was not cut suddenly or by force. We were growing apart, heading in a new direction as we decided our future, while our relatives' lives continued to evolve around festivals in the Christian calendar, including christenings, confirmations, and weddings.

By the time we made *aliyah* we had been carefully uprooted from this lifestyle and were ready to be planted anew in a fresh, spiritually rich environment, fertile and enriching for our hungry souls.

At the *Merkaz Klita*, the Jewish Outreach Center in Ra'anana organized evening and morning prayer services every Shabbat. Rabbi Weiss usually gave a sermon in English, but the prayers were, naturally, in Hebrew. It was all so different and new to me. Still, I found the services fascinating and somehow satisfying, although I did not know much about prayer in a *Beit Knesset*. This was our first Jewish community. In Finland we did not live among Jews, nor did we attend synagogue on a regular basis, simply because there wasn't one where we lived during the years we were turning towards Judaism. The closest we had ever lived to a synagogue was in Australia, ten years earlier. To my regret I never visited the synagogue in Brisbane, although we were neighbors on Bunya Street. Hopefully, one day, I will knock on the door of the Bunya Street Synagogue.

How many times have I envied Jewish children who have the privilege of attending a religious kindergarten and school, and who receive practical and theoretical training in the faith from an early age. Not to mention what they receive from their guiding parents. It is a wonderful sight to see parents teaching their children the blessings before eating, or explaining the Torah portion for the week. Slowly I began to understand the meaning of *Kabbalat Shabbat* (Friday evening service which marks the entrance of Shabbat), praying with a *minyan* (a quorum of ten Jewish men needed for a public prayer service), and so on. But the learning would take a long time. I stepped into the *Beit Knesset* of the *Merkaz Klita*, and I longed to be a part of it, but knew so little of the practices.

One of my favorite tasks as a minister was leading a service. Already during my studies, I had earned top grades in liturgical song; I knew how to conduct a service with a blend of solemnity, dignity, and joy. While in Australia I was a member of the liturgical committee of the Lutheran Church of Queensland. In Finland I was selected to be among the ministers who regularly broadcast services, including sermons on national radio and TV. Yet here I was in a service where I could not even read through the Hebrew prayers without help. And I was supposed to have found my place, to have come home and been fulfilled? Although it was not easy, I was not disappointed.

I was called up to the *bimah* for my first *aliyah* to the Torah. A *bimah* is the raised platform from where the Torah scroll is read. When you immigrate to Israel you "make *aliyah*," in literal terms, you "ascend" to Israel. The same term is used during the synagogue service when a person receives the honor of being called up to the Torah. This was my first *aliyah* to the Torah. The *chazzan* (cantor) had to help me through the blessing in Hebrew.

I'm sure I made a fool of myself, but everybody was kind to me. I swallowed my pride, because no matter how new and strange it all was, my soul was satisfied. I was a part of something, I belonged somewhere. I was attached to a lifeline for my spiritual survival. "Now you are a full member of the House of Israel." The words of Rabbi Michael in Helsinki, with whom we converted, rang beautifully in my ears. I had to begin to practice that new life even if it was difficult and time-consuming.

The sense of fulfillment and the answers to my questions did not come to me at once, but I knew this was the right place for me. I also knew that I had done the right thing. I felt I had been rescued from a sinking ship; I was happy just to be alive. Now I could begin to live again. There was no rush – it was too late to be in a hurry. I would devote the rest of my life to my new soul, to discovering my new path. Remembering my awful dream, in which I was about to die a spiritual death, I now felt very much alive and well. To convert and to make *aliyah*, to make the shift from being a respected minister to a novice Jew at kindergarten level, requires a huge portion of humility – so huge, that at times it felt like self-denial.

In larger terms, there was an aspect of dying and of rebirth. My old self had to die. The old me had to be denied, held back. Left to wither in peace. This part of the process required an enormous amount of self-restraint and humility. I had to accept the fact that my old life was over. Everything I knew best was now useless. I did not need to know how to conduct a Christian Church service anymore. A conversion is like a "soul transplant." My new soul was my new life. Now it was my duty to care for the well-being of my Jewish soul. I had experienced a rebirth, I was a new person, a kindergarten student starting from the very beginning. The only difference was that I was in my forties.

After we moved out of the *Merkaz Klita* to another part of town, we started to look for a *Beit Knesset* we could call our own. One Shabbat, our good friends Ed and Eileen Nadler invited us to a newly established *kehilla* with a young and enthusiastic rabbi and rebbetzin, Kinor David with Rabbi Tzvi and Oshra Koren. In this warm, open, and happy *Kehilla*, we found our place. The captivating tunes of Rabbi Shlomo Carlebach echoed during the Shabbat prayer service, welcoming people to join in. At Kinor David, there were no reserved seats. Anyone, anytime, was welcome to attend. This was exactly what we needed. We were welcomed wholeheartedly, and a seat was always available for us. Back in Finland we had not experienced much shared joy at our conversion. Our fragile new souls did not know what to expect in our new environment. How surprised we were when we slowly opened up and were met with such a welcome. At last, somebody was rejoicing at our conversion. We began to feel more at home.

We still had one more surprise awaiting us. It began when Rabbi Tzvi asked about our conversion in Helsinki. He wanted to know exactly how we did it, what was involved, if Ruth and I were married according to Jewish *halacha*, among other things. These questions made me feel uncomfortable. If it had not been for his friendly smile and eyes glowing with warmth and humility, I would have become upset. Still, I did not understand why he questioned the conversion that was accepted by the State of Israel. Our Israeli ID stated "Jew" under nationality. We had documents to prove it, signed by the Orthodox Chief Rabbi of Helsinki, with the stamp of the *Beit Din* of Helsinki. (A *Beit Din* is a three-member court of rabbis who rule on issues such as conversion.) It took me a while to realize that this line of questioning was symptomatic of a culture that was still so new to us, a culture where you have the right, and even the responsibility, to question everything, from how often and where you pray, to what kind of food you eat. In our previous way of life these issues were private, not often discussed. Our adjustment to this different culture would take time.

Ruth and I had not been married under a *chuppah* (a canopy under which Jewish marriages take place) in Helsinki. Rabbi Tzvi was alarmed. According to Jewish law, we were not married. I certainly had not realized this. I only knew that Rabbi Michael in Helsinki left to take up another position the day after we received our conversion papers. Consequently nothing was done about any further procedures. And we had already begun planning our move to Israel.

"We'd better check with Jerusalem, to make sure your conversion is filed with the Rabbinate in Israel, not only with the Ministry of Interior. That's not enough," Rabbi Tzvi explained. Suddenly a chilling feeling of uncertainty came over me. What if it wasn't enough? What then? "Anyway, we have to make sure you get married under the *chuppah* as soon as possible, and for that we need the approval of the Rabbinate. So that will be one way of finding out." Rabbi Tzvi was comforting, but he could not hide his suspicion that there might still be a long way to go. "What if it is not registered?" I pressed him. What then?

"There are two possibilities," he replied. "Either they accept your

Helsinki conversion as it is or you have to make a new conversion here in Israel."

For a moment, I was speechless. "There is a possibility that we have to undergo the conversion process again?"

"The best way to find out is to set a meeting with them as soon as possible."

I remember my disappointment that bordered on anger. What about the rabbi's declaration in Helsinki welcoming us into the House of Israel? How happy I was to hear that statement. Had I received a Jewish soul or not? How many times can you become a Jew? We had just started to enjoy the fruits of our conversion, as we were welcomed into our new community as Jews. I was just about to learn to walk when I was pushed over. And again, I had to take it from the beginning.

A meeting was scheduled for a few weeks later with a representative of the Rabbinate of Jerusalem. Rabbi Tzvi, who had made the initial contact, joined us for the trip and made the official introductions, but only my wife and myself met with the rabbi. The representative listened to our story and kindly asked a few test questions. But his mind seemed to have been made up. He rejected us. The reason, as we understood it, was that he did not know the Helsinki Chief Rabbi well enough. And also, for our own good, the family was asked to study and take a new test some time at a later date. To me it did not matter if it was tomorrow or in a year; the fact that he sowed doubt in my soul as to who I was, and doubt regarding the previous conversion – an event that meant so much to me – was a heavy enough burden for the moment. Was the joy and fulfillment I had felt over becoming a Jew unjustified? Maybe I wasn't a Jew yet? I grieved as if I had lost somebody. I grieved over the Jewish soul he had taken away from me. Was it really up to him to take it or give it? My questions were charged with heavy emotions, which I shared with my wife, who also felt the loss keenly.

We knew what we had to do. We both wanted to regain our lost souls as soon as possible. Meanwhile, we had to confront our daughters with the situation and this was an enormous source of pain and grief for us. How much could they take? I asked myself again.

It turned out to be as difficult as I feared it would. The two youngest, Karolin and Josefin, who were only fourteen years old at the time, were enrolled in a secular school with special classes for new immigrants. This was not acceptable for the Rabbinate. They had to change to a religious school with religious subjects, otherwise none of us could continue studying with the hope of being accepted for conversion.

Fearing a situation of being without a valid religious status, so important for their Jewish marriage, the girls hesitantly agreed to move to the school advised by the Rabbinate. They also started a learning program helpfully organized by our congregation.

At this time our congregation, Kinor David, came to our rescue. Throughout our difficulties and our doubts, they were eager to reassure us how they felt and how they regarded us. To them we were Jews. The support from Rabbi Tzvi and Oshra helped us gain the right perspective. Joining the Jewish fold means a lifetime of commitment and learning. I never disagreed with that, but I would have preferred the first conversion to have been accepted. Our learning would continue anyway. Does it have to come the hardest possible way? If we had only known earlier that many of the conversions performed abroad must be completed in Israel, it might have softened the blow somewhat.

The next year was scheduled with learning sessions for all of us. My *hevruta* was Rabbi Menahem Sela. His practical outlook was very much to my liking, yet when necessary, we could also dig deep into philosophical questions. There were other people who dedicated their precious time, providing us with guidance about what it means to be a Jew. Willie Malkinson and Daniel Blaukopf, members of our community, gave their input in our learning as well. I should know so much, since I had so many excellent teachers! My daughters and my wife had their learning sessions with Malki Swidler, another member of Kinor David, and every so often Rabbi Tzvi met with all of us to monitor our progress and provide his feedback.

A year later we mustered the courage to approach the Rabbinate again. We passed some initial tests before we were sent to the three-member court for our final test. Initially it should have been held in Jerusalem, but a last-minute change of plans ordered us to go to a *Beit Din* in the North to meet with the local Rabbinate headed by the Chief Rabbi.

Not knowing what to expect, we were understandably nervous. Three of our daughters, Sara, 17, Karolin and Josefin, both 14, my wife, Ruth and I made the trip. Our eldest daughter, Linda, 19, chose to attend another year-long conversion class and was going to take her test soon with a different Rabbinate. Our meeting was set for nine o'clock in the morning.

We began the long drive at sunrise, at about six o'clock. The scenery was beautiful, with the rolling hills and valleys as our background, but the view was the last thing on our minds. Instead we were repeating the *brachot* (blessings), asking ourselves questions about reward and punishment, such as, what happens to the soul after death? The questions were endless. Yet we seemed to know the answers. The girls proudly listed by heart the thirteen principles of faith. The only question we did not seem to have an answer for was not about life after death, but rather: life after the test? Will they accept us? What will be their attitude? Will it be a humiliating or encouraging experience?

One by one we entered the small office of the court. I was called in first. The Chief Rabbi addressed me in his soft, friendly tone, which calmed me down. Maybe I didn't need to be nervous after all. He offered me a drink and biscuits. I assumed this was part of the test to see if I knew the correct *bracha*. So far so good, I thought, after reciting the proper blessings. He asked my wife to join me. "So tell me your story, it seems to be quite unusual," he said. That gave me the opportunity I was waiting for. If I could just tell him about our desire, dedication, and readiness to live a Jewish life, that would convince him more than anything else. I had seen how, in Judaism, the answer to a tricky question could be debated endlessly without any agreement about which answer was the correct one. The rabbi could either accept or fail you, regardless of the answer. The decision was his alone. I desperately wanted to avoid that kind of situation. Now he had given me the perfect opportunity to talk about our story. And I did it with fire in my eyes and conviction in my voice. Suddenly it was as if the clock was turned back to my first meeting with Rabbi Michael in Helsinki. It was a question of gaining confidence, getting the message across, convincing him of our sincerity. The Chief Rabbi listened. I stopped halfway to see whether to continue or not. He was still with me, he nodded for me to go on. I looked sideways to check Ruth's reactions. I knew she was happy that I was doing most of the talking. At the end the Chief Rabbi turned to her, to make sure she agreed. When it comes to her conviction, Ruth is perfectly capable of speaking for herself, but now she only had to agree. That was enough.

Before he let us go, he asked Ruth some questions about *kashrut*. What kind of scales does a fish need to have to be kosher? "Scales that come off easily like on salmon and not like crayfish which is not kosher." Her answer seemed to have been accepted. "By the way, Shlomo, what do you think about the Moshiach?" he asked, when we were already on the way out. Of course he wanted to check my opinion on that issue, as a former Christian minister. I believe that we agreed on the answer. But still he did not give a clear indication about what his decision would be. We went out and waited for our daughters to complete their tests.

One by one, Sara, Karolin, and Josefin emerged in tears. They did not believe they even stood a chance. They told the collected forum of rabbis why they wanted to become Jews. They answered questions about *kashrut*, blessings, and principles of faith. Why do we celebrate Pesach, Shavuot, and Sukkot? What is the significance of Hannukah? They answered, they talked, because they wanted so much to be accepted.

Once they had their turns, all that was left to do was to wait for the verdict. The secretary of the *Beit Din* called us in. This time they wanted to see all of us together. The Chief Rabbi explained, "I was fascinated by the parents' story, and I see no other choice but to accept them into the Jewish faith, but for the girls, I have come to another decision. They are still not ready. To be a Jew requires a lot. I want them to know as much as my daughter. I therefore suggest that you continue studying and come back before Pesach."

I could not believe it. This separation between parents and children was too much for us to take. Hadn't we shared everything, hadn't we moved towards the same goals, and made the same decisions? The rabbis even spoke of the difficulties we would face, living in the same household, since my wife and I would be Jews and our daughters non-Jews. For instance, a Jew cannot eat food prepared by a non-Jew, therefore we should not eat the food prepared by our children.

We left this northern town and its Rabbinate feeling despondent and full of grief. There was no reason for Ruth and I to celebrate since our daughters couldn't share our joy.

The girls studied hard for another confrontation with the *Beit Din*. Pesach was approaching and the next meeting was scheduled. This time I could not attend. Only Ruth and our daughters headed north. One by one they faced the panel of rabbis for questioning. There seemed to be a similar attitude this time. The girls emerged once again in tears. Another humiliating moment. "We cannot accept you. Please, come again." They cried all the way home.

I was lost for words when Ruth called to tell me the news. I was

devastated, thinking of how the girls would face this bitter disappointment. I knew that they were strong, but still there was a limit to how much
they could take. A strong wave of guilt came over me. What have I done?
The girls did not deserve this treatment. How can I ever ask them to do
anything again for the sake of being Jewish? Not that I needed to; they
knew for themselves how important it was to have matters in order with
the Rabbinate. But still, the questions came to me: How can they find the
motivation after this setback? How can they see the beauty of Judaism,
when dealt this kind of harsh treatment? I did not know how to console
my daughters, and they were not easily comforted. A deep disappointment
that verged on rebellion entered their young minds.

I tried to look at it from another perspective. Judaism does not seek
out converts. The convert himself has to ask over and over again to be accepted. This is a symbol of the high demands Judaism places on its followers.
It is not an easy religion, so why should it be easy to enter into it?

If there were tears at the meeting when we left the Church, many
years earlier, so there were tears also when we were accepted into Judaism.
The girls decided that they had nothing more to lose, so one more time
before the Rabbinate was worth a try. We booked into a bed and breakfast
hotel near the Rabbinate's office. The Chief Rabbi himself visited us during
our last-minute learning. We were hoping the tension might ease a little,
making the test less trying for the girls. The Rabbinate had rejected us, but
we had the chutzpah to return each time. With this fighting spirit, Sara,
Karolin, and Josefin tried once more.

The third time, they were accepted. It had not been a pleasant experience, but they had made it. No welcoming into the House of Israel; not a
single word of consolation or encouragement. Judaism is so much more
beautiful than the lessons we learned at the *Beit Din*. I realize that our
conversion had to be accepted by the Religious Authorities in Israel, but
the question remains if it had to be this hard? Had it not been for Rabbi
Tzvi and his curious questions, this issue might have erupted the day our
daughters wanted to get married. I'd rather have it this way, where nobody
can doubt the validity of our conversion, and our daughters agree. Thank
you, Rav Tzvi.

We had proven ourselves in our stubborn perseverance. The tree that
had been uprooted from another faith was finally replanted. Maybe this
time, it would be allowed time to grow strong and tall, resisting the wind

and storms to come. Our daughters felt hurt for a long time. Somewhere deep in their soul there is a scar that will take a long time to heal. But nevertheless their Jewish identity is growing stronger and Israel has become their home. By now Linda, our oldest daughter, had also passed her conversion test after attending a year-long course.

Finally we received our documents from the *Beit Din* declaring us to be members of the House of Israel. No wonder a good friend and neighbor jokingly calls us "certifiably crazy."

A few years after the difficult experience of our second conversion, traumatic memories of the *Beit Din* continue to haunt our daughters from time to time. Yet comfort takes many forms. Rabbi Pinhas HaCohen Wilman in Petach Tikvah is a Rambam scholar and has published, among others, a book titled, *Orot HaRambam* ("Rambam" from the acronym of Rabbi Moses ben Maimon, who lived from 1138 to 1204). In his book Rabbi Wilman published a letter by Rambam written as consolation to a convert who was insulted by his teacher. Rambam writes how God Himself loves a person who left his former way of life and worship, in order to start a new life as a member of the House of Israel. Nobody is allowed to ridicule this person. Ovadia, the original recipient of Rambam's letter, was also reminded of the reward that God will bestow upon the convert.

Rambam's letter, written some 800 years ago, brought perspective to our conversion. What does the attitude of men matter if God, the Almighty Maker of heaven and earth, is pleased by the fact that somebody has turned to Him? The main religions of the world have all copied fragments of Judaism, left some aspects aside, and turned others upside down. Therefore, when somebody returns to Judaism it is a reason to show respect and it is a source of joy. This message seems to have been of great importance to Rambam. Despite his very hectic schedule as a physician, philosopher, and scholar he took the time to write a letter to comfort a hurt convert.

FIFTEEN

Young Love

SARA, OUR SECOND-OLDEST daughter, who had left a boyfriend behind in Finland, was trying to come to terms with her feelings about finding her soul mate. She had already given one up in Finland, and was afraid that she would not find again what she had already lost. Sara is lovable, affectionate, happy, and sociable, like a golden retriever, always looking for company, and the drastic move hit her especially hard.

One *Motzei Shabbat* (Saturday night) Sara asked her sisters to join her for a trip to Jerusalem. She is brimming with initiative, always wanting to go places and meet people. This time, they went to a café, popular with the crowds of young people. Little did Sara know what that evening would bring – expectations and hope, but even more so, broken illusions and tears.

A handsome, tall, young man entered the cafe. The girls noticed him the way young women do. What Sara did not know then was that Amiram came there that evening hoping to meet somebody special. He couldn't help but notice the blond girls and he said to his friends half jokingly, half seriously, looking at Sara: "God sent her to me tonight." Coming to his senses, he continued to reflect on the face he just saw. "She is for sure a tourist and probably not Jewish, so I'd better not get my hopes up," Amiram said to his friends, who were sitting at a nearby table, making eye contact with the girls.

This was not the girls' first visit to Jerusalem. Often, when they wanted to go out, they found Jerusalem an interesting place, and we certainly had nothing against it. On the contrary, we thought Jerusalem was the place to be when it came to meeting new friends. Hoping that our girls would find decent, religious Jewish boys, but unfamiliar with the tradition of "match-making," we've left it to the girls themselves to look for partners. That's not to say we do not care or express our opinion; my wife in particular is adept at making her opinion known on this issue. Somehow her advice is not always well received, but it is there anyway for free. That's the "Yiddishe Mama" in her who wants to select her daughter's future husband, rather than leave this important task to the young and inexperienced.

The Brunell sisters and Amiram and his friends were still seated at separate tables. Eye contact had already communicated what words just had to confirm. Before long, the two groups were seated around the same table, animated in a lively discussion. Sara's green eyes were sparkling – she was happy to be talking to somebody so attractive and pleasant, who was seeking her attention. Before they knew it, it was already late and time to go. "So can we meet again?" Amiram asked, "or are you leaving soon?" Finding out that Sara lived in Israel, and was an *Olah Hadashah*, startled Amiram. "What if God really sent her to me," he thought.

A week later, at the same place, Sara and Amiram met to get to know each other better. The conversation seemed to flow with ease. This was a good sign. Sara and Amiram had a lot to talk about. They continued to meet and got to know each other better. Love was in the air, although their backgrounds were worlds apart. Amiram, born in Israel to Iranian parents, had just finished his *yeshiva* studies and was ready to join the army. *Yeshiva* is a Jewish school for Torah studies. He was dark and tall, with the stature of a king. Sara, blond like a birch tree in the Scandinavian summer, was about to graduate from college, and was new to Israel, new to her faith, and waiting for her soul mate. As Jerusalem is the focal point for the Jewish faith and unites Jewish souls, so these two had met in the Holy City from such different backgrounds. The two young hearts started to hope it would be for a reason.

Amiram told his mother about Sara. His voice sounded happy; he talked like a man in love. This is the moment when every mother listens carefully. Who is this person capturing my son's heart? The family was traditionally religious, knowledgeable in the *halacha*, the Jewish law that guides Jewish life down to its smallest detail. Amiram was a *yeshiva* student, very popular both among his friends and teachers, but there was one lesson he had failed to remember from his studies, and his mother was quick to remind him of it. Sara is fine, there is nothing wrong with her, and there are many heroines among the converts who joined the Jewish faith. "The problem is not Sara, the problem is you," Amiram's mother reminded him. "A Jew from any other tribe can marry a convert, but you are a *Cohen* and a Jew belonging to the priestly line of Aaron is not allowed to marry a convert." There at the kitchen table, Amiram sank deep into his chair, covered his eyes with his hands and shed bitter tears. He was a strong young man, but how was he supposed to react? His heart broke in an instant; the pain was equal to the sorrow of losing somebody.

His mother shared his pain. This was not a matter to be taken lightly. Amiram knew that there was no future for him and Sara. His sorrow paved the way for a few poems; he already had hundreds of them in his collection. Poetic and sensitive, he gathered strength from his writing and many more lines floated from his pen before he summoned the courage to call Sara.

"Sara, there is a phone call for you," her sister called out. When Sara went into her room to talk we heard her voice becoming softer and softer. Half an hour later she emerged, tears running down her cheeks. "But we decided to remain friends," she concluded her story. Still, the hurt remained with her a long time. As Sara's parents, we also grieved for her, grieved for the consequences of the far-reaching decisions that we had brought upon our daughters.

Sara and Amiram have remained friends, and he also remains a family friend. Often, when visiting Jerusalem, he gives us a guided tour through the Old City, or helps find the best deals at the Machane Yehuda market. Turning to Radio Yerushalayim, while in the capital, you might hear one of Amiram's songs being played. He is both a poet and a singer and his debut CD features a song dedicated to Sara. The chorus says it all: "Sorry that I loved you, Sorry that I touched your heart."

When beginning a new life, as we have done, it may feel as if there is not enough time to learn everything anew. This knowledge keeps you humble, and tests your faith and your personality. You are taken to the outer limits of yourself, and for a while, it is not clear whether you will make it. If you do, you come out stronger and wiser, more determined to do the right thing. Nevertheless the emotions are hard to accept. "Sorry that I loved you...."

This hard lesson of life was also learned by our oldest daughter and her fiancé.

There can be obstacles in a relationship, some can't be removed as in the case for Sara and her Cohen friend, while other obstacles can be dealt with. Already before our conversion in Finland Linda had gotten engaged to Nick, whom she had known for some time. Not knowing how the future would take shape for the two of them, Linda joined us on our aliya leaving Nick at the train station waving good-bye. The separation did not last long. Soon Nick was a happy volunteer at a kibbutz not far from our Merkaz Klita. His happiness was more for the reason of being in the same country as his fiancée than for the place where he stayed. Being a business partner with his father back in Finland, the life at the kibbutz was a totally different experience. The situation however was far from solved with that move. As the future would show there were many tough decisions to be made by this young Finnish man and by the two of them together before things settled down. As the options were placed before them they decided to attend a conversion course together. For Nick this was something completely new. Linda, who had converted once already in Finland, had to attend for the same reason as the rest of her family – to get the acceptance of the religious authorities in Israel.

During a period of one year Linda and Nick went to Netanya 4–5 evenings a week. This conversion course was a very intense education, giving spiritual encouragement as well as "building material" for the faith. This course ended with a series of tests, both written and oral. Part of the test was however the duration and intensity of the course. Those not serious enough dropped out during the program. The final test was in front of a three-member rabbinical court. The whole family was in excitement and anticipation about the outcome. How happy we were to see the relief on the faces of the two, Linda and Nick, coming out from the rabbinate. They made it. Linda took the name Lea Hanna and Nick, influenced by the much-loved teacher in the course, chose the name Benjamin as his Hebrew name.

Like pearls on a necklace one after the other, so was the sequence of events following their conversion. There was bureaucracy and the brit mila, more bureaucracy followed by the ritual mikve, followed by the wedding under the hupa.

This all seemed so beautiful and meaningful. How difficult it is to understand that a couple of years later the two divorced and Nick moved back to Finland. But he does not give up his Judaism. Even though it is a lonely Jewish life for him in the small town where he lives, he struggles hard to keep up and practice his newly gained faith.

"Sorry that I loved you, sorry that I touched your heart…"

SIXTEEN

A Gift from Up Above

AN ISRAELI YOUNGSTER approaches his father after completing his three years of service in the IDF (Israeli Defense Force). As do so many others, this young man wants to travel, gain independence, and see the world. But there is more to this traveling experience than just the freedom after a long and intensive army service; there is a search for identity, a search for the soul. The young man says to his father: "I'm traveling to India, I need to go and find myself."

"But here you are, my son," the father replies. "You don't need to go and look for yourself, you are right here."

This partly sarcastic response by the father also reveals a very impor-tant, but oft-neglected, truth. As a Jew, you don't need to look anywhere but to your own religion to find yourself. My family and I came from afar to find what every Jew already has. The Torah given to the Jews is our life manual, it is a guide for the whole of mankind. Other nations have adopted parts of it as their guidelines. The nations of the world seek guidance from the Jewish code, but a Jew does not need to go anywhere else but to his own roots to find himself, and to find the best available guidelines for life.

"Our Torah was not given to individuals, not to the angels and not to the gentile nations. It was addressed to the nation, which stood at Mt. Sinai, the entire spiritual community of Israel, past, present and future" (Rabbi Kook in *Eretz Yisrael*). The secrets of God are there, waiting to be discovered. The Torah can be found in your own home or in the nearest *Beit Knesset*. Through the Torah your soul will come alive. Your questions will be answered. Your appetite will grow, and you will find that the well is deep and the bread is fresh.

In Isaiah (55:1–2), we read: "Come all who are thirsty, come to the waters, and you who have no money come buy and eat! Come buy wine and milk without money and without cost. Why spend money on what is not bread and your labor on what does not satisfy. Listen, listen to me and eat what is good, and your soul will delight in the richest of fare."

If the connection between the People and the Torah is obvious, so is the connection between the People and the Land. Just as God gave the Torah to His People, so too did He give them the Land.

It is puzzling that so many Jews can still live outside of their homeland, Israel. New York is no substitute for Jerusalem. Why be satisfied with second-best when you can have the best? I believe it's only a matter of time before we will witness another massive *aliyah*, from Europe, South America, South Africa, the US, Australia, Asia, from every corner of the world where Jews can be found. I believe so, because it is written in Jeremiah (23:5–8): "The days are coming, declares the Lord, when I will raise up to David a righteous Branch, a King who will reign wisely and do what is just and right in the land. In his days Judah will be saved and Israel will live in safety. This is the name by which he will be called The Lord Our Righteousness. So then the days are coming, declares the Lord, when people will no longer say, 'As surely as the Lord lives who brought the Israelites up out of Egypt,' but they will say, 'As surely as the Lord lives, who brought the descendants of Israel up out of the land of the north and out of all the countries where he had banished them.' Then they will live in their own land."

In accordance with these words of the prophet Jeremiah, the coming exodus will be comparable to the Exodus from Egypt. This will be the magnitude of the *aliyah* to Israel that we have yet to witness. What amazes me is that my family and I, as strangers, were also part of this plan. Indeed, people of all languages and tongues have joined the chosen people throughout history. In fact, during the first Exodus from Egypt, many native Egyptians joined the battered people and followed them in their newly-won freedom to the desert, en route to their own Land. I read sections of the Tanach in which prophets discuss foreigners who learn about the Shabbat and learn to love the name of Hashem, and how these people are allowed to join the community of Israel, finding joy and fulfillment in their prayers.

"And foreigners who bind themselves to the Lord to serve him, to love the name of the Lord and to worship Him, all who keep the Shabbat without desecrating it and who hold fast to My covenant, these I will bring to My holy mountain and give them joy in My house of prayer" (Isaiah 56:6–8).

Our family received a gift from the Almighty, the greatest gift. We accepted it and to our great joy we were also received with love. The odds of a successful *aliyah* were stacked against us. Seven years after our first experience at the *Merkaz Klita*, life is still not easy but we are settled in our new homeland. We work very hard to make a living, as do most Israelis. We do not reflect on the alternatives; we are here to stay.

Our daughters are busy, their days filled with work and study. Linda has chosen a career as a paralegal and is working in a patent law office. Sara is studying graphic design and her spare time is dedicated to horses, which are her great interest. Sara's comment recently about living in Israel was simply: "I live here because I'm a Jew." Karolin has finished her two years of army service in the Israeli Air Force. Her dream is to become a pilot and she has made a good start by studying at a flight school while working at Teva medical company. Her twin sister Josefin is working for Kodak Company while pursuing studies in photography, which she hopes to turn into a professional career. My wife Ruth went into real estate and is now working with Re/Max as a real estate agent.

Our greatest realization is that we are a part of the biblical prophecies that are being fulfilled in our time. The establishment of the State of Israel is one amazing step in the series of events leading up to the coming of Moshiach, and the arrival of each and every *Oleh Hadash / Olah Hadashah* brings us one step closer to the fulfillment of God's master plan. This overwhelming feeling struck me on our first night at the *Merkaz Klita*, and I derived great comfort in the knowledge that God is trustworthy. He fulfills what He promises. The Almighty's plan is carried out to the smallest detail. Maybe our family was one of these small details. The God of Israel is about to establish the Kingdom of David. He needs His people to be here, in His Land, in order for it to happen. God will not crown His King with most of His people absent.

The whole concept of a Savior, a Moshiach, is, of course, Jewish, not Christian. Jews throughout history have always resolutely believed in the coming of the Moshiach. During hard times, the longing for the Moshiach has sustained the Jews, providing hope for the future. In ancient times, and in more recent days, the promise that one day the Davidic dynasty will provide the Messianic King has influenced the very identity of the Jewish people. During the last few political elections in Israel, some campaign slogans have stated their trust in a particular politician who is promising to deliver peace and stability. One slogan said: "Rak (only) Barak." Another slogan said: "Rak (only) Sharon." Shortly afterwards a new poster appeared with the message: "Rak (only) Moshiach." There is no other nation that longs and prays for the Moshiach as passionately and wholeheartedly as the Jews. Three times a day, during the morning, afternoon, and evening prayers, every religious Jew prays for the rebuilding of Jerusalem and the reestablishment of the Davidic dynasty and salvation through the coming of Moshiach. In the twelfth beautiful principle of faith, the Jews declare: "I believe with complete faith in the coming of the Moshiach, and even though he may delay, nevertheless I anticipate every day that he will come."

The Jewish Moshiach does not need a second chance (read: "second coming"). He will do it right the first time around. When he comes he will be a person of the tribe of Yehudah, as was King David, and therefore we talk about the Davidic line. He will be conceived and born as a normal human being. He will be appointed King and will reign in Jerusalem; he will establish peace in Israel, in the Middle East and throughout the world. We will experience not only a temporary cease-fire, but a real and lasting peace, that will be recognized by all. The Third Temple will be established in its rightful place on the Temple Mount in Jerusalem. The righteous dead will be restored to life and a time of Messianic tranquility will be established on earth. Jerusalem will be the center of worship. Every nation will be eager to send delegations to the new Temple to take part in celebrations and festivals. The God of Israel, who made His name known to our forefathers, will be recognized by all nations as the only God of the entire universe. This is all worth waiting for. Worth the longing and praying. Even the suffering and the hardships will be seen in a new light.

In Isaiah (2:2–5), we read: "In the last days the mountain of the Lord's temple will be established as chief among the mountains, it will be raised above the hills and all the nations will stream to it. Many peoples will come and say, 'Come let us go up to the mountain of the Lord, to the house of the God of Jacob. He will teach us His ways, so that we may walk in His paths.' The law will go out from Zion, the word of God from Jerusalem. He will judge between the nations and will settle disputes for many peoples. They will beat their swords into plowshares and their spears into pruning hooks.

Nation will not take up sword against nation, nor will they train for war anymore. Come, O house of Jacob, let us walk in the light of the Lord."

A Jew is deeply rooted in history, because there his religion is manifest. He is also a visionary because he believes in the future. He can look back and he can also cast his eyes to the horizon. He is sure of his history, convinced that the God of his fathers, the only God, will draw His children close and bring to fruition the promises He showed to the prophets.

Israel is a beautiful land and the people are special, because God has chosen them one by one to live in this Land. When I walk down the street I sometimes stop in my tracks, and take a minute to notice the people around me. They all seem so different, speaking so many different languages, yet seeing them all as Jews fills me with a deep warmth. We are all family and *Eretz Yisrael* is the catalyst that brings us together. This is what makes the difference. There are many factors, some that may seem very small, that impact on a person's decision to move to Israel. A South-African businessman told me of his experience. He had two options, either to move to the USA or to Israel. To help him decide, he came on a pilot tour to Israel. "When even the taxi drivers greet you with *Shabbat Shalom* on Friday afternoon – that tipped it for me in favor of Israel." He came and he stayed. In Ra'anana, I met Ilan, a photographer, who had travelled to Australia and fallen in love with it. There he met a non-Jewish girl, whom he began dating, until one day he realized – I want my children to call me "Abba." He moved back home to Israel and today he has a Jewish wife, and children who call him "Abba." The small things in life can make a big difference.

God's pull comes in many forms. Ultimately the Torah brings people to Israel. Similarly the Land will also bring people to the Torah, because the Torah and the Land are connected. One cannot exist without the other. And both belong to the Jewish people. *HaMakom* (a synonym for "God" – the "Omnipresent") calls His people to His *Makom* (translates literally as "place"). The union of the TORAH, the LAND and the PEOPLE will be a blessing for all the nations of the world. This blessing will be greater than anything the nations have ever seen before, as we learn from Isaiah 2, quoted above. We will finally arrive at *Shalom* – Peace.

Anyone familiar with the Bible will know the beautiful story of Joseph's emotional reunion with his brothers, after revealing his identity to them (Genesis 45). Today, we anticipate the moment when there will be real unity among all the brethren of Israel. We will see an era of peace under a king from the House of David, who will be a servant of God and will unify the people in their allegiance to the Torah. The thrilling outcome will be that the whole world will know that Hashem is God and Israel is His chosen people.

Israel as a nation was looked upon with jealousy and suspicion by other nations, in the same way as Joseph was the object of such emotions in the eyes of his brothers. This enmity reached its climax when the people of Israel were thrown into the gas chambers during the Holocaust. Miraculously Israel emerged back on the scene, strong and confident, yet still not universally recognized as God's special people, who brought the Torah to the world. But the moment will arrive when God's glory will be manifested in the midst of Israel. There was shock and confusion among the brothers when Joseph, having emerged from the pit and having been made viceroy of Egypt, revealed his identity to them. Can you imagine the perplexed reaction of all the enemies of Israel on the day when God decides to manifest his glory once again in Jerusalem and reveal His connection to Israel? At the time that God will make himself known, also Israel will be recognized as His people, because all these elements fit together – Hashem and His people in the Land that He gave. And all this will take place right here in *Eretz Yisrael*.

What really matters for a Jew is to be in *Eretz Yisrael*, and to work towards the achievement of unity amongst our people. The divisions that we experience today existed already in the sons of Jacob. There was Yehuda, who did not even care about selling his brother Joseph. Joseph, on the other hand, was studying Torah at his father's *yeshiva*. Unfortunately, as a young shepherd, Joseph gave evil reports about his brothers to their father, fueling the bad feelings between them. How distant they were from one another! And yet the brothers conciliated years later. By the end of their trials before Joseph, then the viceroy of Egypt, Yehuda steps forward in a stunning petition, offering himself as a slave instead of Benjamin – showing remorse for the wrongdoings against Joseph. Not until the brethren had set aside their jealousies and internal struggles were they ready for reconciliation. The brothers became one in spirit and soul. "We are sons of one man," the brothers declared to Joseph.

The Jewish people are approaching the time for reconciliation. We must focus on the things that unite us. Our Holy Torah, the Shabbat, *Eretz Yisrael*, Yerushalayim…we are the people of the one God. Our heritage must bring us together. This goal is depicted beautifully in the *haftara* for *Vayigash* (*Haftara* is the weekly prophet reading in the synagogue and *Vayigash* is the specific name of one of the Torah readings. *Vayigash* is Genesis 44:18–47:27): "My servant David will be king over them, and there will be a single shepherd for all of them; they will go in My ordinances and they will observe My decrees and perform them. They will dwell on the land that I gave to My servant Jacob, within which your forefathers dwelt and they shall dwell upon it – they, their children and their children's children, forever; and My servant David will be prince over them, forever."

"I shall seal a covenant of peace with them, an eternal covenant shall it be with them; and I shall emplace them and I shall increase them, and I shall place My Sanctuary among them forever. My dwelling place shall be upon them, and I shall be a God unto them, and they shall be unto Me for a people. Then the nations shall know that I am Hashem, Who sanctifies Israel, when My Sanctuary is among them forever" (Ezekiel 37:24–28).

SEVENTEEN

Not Just A Wedding, But A Completion

WHILE WE HAD been "battling" with the Rabbinate to gain our conversion, our friends in Kinor David had been secretly planning our *chuppah*. Our long overdue Jewish wedding took place on Lag BaOmer of 2000. Lag BaOmer is a Jewish festival that takes place on the 18th of the month of *Iyar*; it usually falls in May and is a popular choice as a day for weddings. In the beautiful garden of our friends, the Inselberg family, my wife and I celebrated the most memorable event we had ever shared together. The wedding stood in total contrast to all the disputes and disappointments – we felt as if we had been lifted to heaven. We were treated to such a wonderful surprise – we only had to prepare ourselves, provide a list of invitations, and to be there. The rest was taken care of: the band, the food, the cameramen, the bar man, the *chuppah*, its four poles held one each by our four daughters.

In case I have given the impression that the Rabbinate suddenly became easier to deal with, let me describe the bureaucracy that was involved before our wedding day. Obviously we had to obtain the right papers in order to get married. At least we had proof of our Jewishness. But there was more. When you enter into a marriage, it is expected that you be single. Here we faced a clear difficulty. It said in our Israeli ID cards that we were married. Now we suddenly had to prove that we were not married. Not to each other, not to anybody else. What could we do? We were sent to a *Beit Din*, this time in Netanya. Standing before a three-member court yet again, I was asked, "How many times a day do you pray?" Here we go again, I thought to myself. Every time we approached yet another authority, who wanted to start from the very beginning. "We really came only to get our marriage documents," I explained. "I understand, but we need a little background." The rabbi answered through his long black beard. He sounded friendly. I decided to be neither too serious nor nervous. We were planning our wedding! There was no reason to get upset. Yet again, I told our story. For the rabbis, however, it was the first time. The atmosphere was positive, and no one even thought of questioning the validity of our case. The security officer who was translating seemed to be doing a good job, although his translation sounded so much longer than my original statement. I am not sure if this was because he was excited to relate my words or whether he felt they needed further elaboration – whatever the reason, it worked. After what turned out to be a pleasant meeting, the Rabbinate assured us that our important document would be sent to Ra'anana in time for our wedding on Lag BaOmer.

The big day arrived. A Jewish wedding is like Yom Kippur for the bride and groom. They prepare themselves by going to the *mikvah* and fasting until after the *chuppah* ceremony. Their sins are forgiven; it is a new beginning, they are like angels in heaven. And certainly we felt like angels. The sense of holiness enveloping me on this day was something that I had felt only once before in my life, after my *brit milah*. Then, I remember, I had also felt as if I had been wrapped in a holy blanket as I was recovering from the *Mohel*'s cut.

We loved the choice of music. Chaim David and his band entertained the guests with their catchy Carlebach-style tunes, while we were inside signing the *Ketuba*. Rabbi Ishon and Rabbi Koren officiated at the ceremony. My *hevruta* Rabbi Sela read the *Ketuba*. My best men were Rabbi Koren and Shlomo Swidler. At this moment I was freed of all the disappointments and sorrows of the past. Stepping out to the green garden, seeing our four daughters smiling happily, holding the poles of the *chuppah*, was a purely joyful and happy experience.

After the *chuppah* and festivities, there were also speeches. First up was Rabbi Tzvi's introduction, and then the floor, or should I say the lawn, was mine.

"What a day, what a moment for us! Thank you all for making it so special.

"How did we reach this moment? Shouldn't this have been done a long time ago? The couple seems to have known each other for a long time. Don't they have grown-up kids already? Yes, you are right. We have known each other for a long time. As a matter of fact we were married twenty-six years ago in Finland. So today, I could say, it's pretty safe to marry someone you know so well. There are no bad surprises, only good ones. And by the way – the kids are from the previous marriage. The story behind all of this is too long to tell now, but briefly I can tell you this:

"We lived in a distant land, another life, in a different world. What I knew about Jewish life and Jews was from the Tanach. I envied the Jewish people because they had a special relationship with God. They were selected from all the nations to be special, to be holy. That's why the Almighty also gave them a Holy Land, a place where they could fulfill this purpose of being special to God and special to the rest of the world. A light to the nations – to show the world the purpose of life.

"And I wanted to be holy; I wanted to have this relationship with God, so even if there was only one chance in a million for me to do it, I would join this holy people. Now I know what you are thinking: we must really have been looking from a long distance if we thought this is what we would find in Israel. Or maybe we had some special glasses that didn't allow us to see the reality. No, I know the reality, I bump into it quite often, but looking around today – what do I see?

"Looking at you now I see a holy people, a people who are looking for opportunities to do *mitzvot* – like you are doing today by joining in our *simcha* [lit., happiness]. Joining the Jewish people means that we can share with you the privilege of keeping the Shabbat, eating kosher food, fasting on Yom Kippur, all the *chagim* [holidays]... the list goes on and on.

"Some fifteen years ago I heard on the news in Finland that the Israeli Airline El Al was about to go bankrupt. I was surprised, but not as surprised as when I found out the decision that was made to make the company profitable again. They decided to stop flying on Shabbat. One of the promises God made to the Jewish people was that if they keep the Shabbat that they won't lose out financially. El Al seems to be a good example. The company quickly became profitable and one of the safest airlines in the world. The lesson from the Shabbat commandment is that God wants to bless us not only spiritually, but also in material terms.

"Soon after our first conversion in Helsinki we chose to make *aliyah*, out of our own free will. That's right, nobody forced us. Australia would have been an easier choice – we lived there for five years. But Israel was our desire. So we came.

"And what a day when we arrived. We came, some four years ago, to the *Merkaz Klita* here in Ra'anana. The first morning we all went to explore the big city. Imagine, coming from Finland in November where you hardly saw the sun. We were not only blond but we were pale, all six of us. We walked out to Ahuza, the main street. With a map in my hand we looked to the right and to the left, wondering where the city center could be. How would we know? Looking at the map (you are not supposed to need a map in a little city like Ra'anana) we decided to go to the right and finally we found a falafel store. I was wondering: why are people looking at us? We are not tourists. We live here. Anyway, from there our life in Israel began.

"Our second conversion was completed a few months ago and now the *chuppah* to make it all official, for nobody to doubt. We want to express our gratitude to all of you, who have been so good to us, so welcoming and so helpful:

"Rabbi Tzvi and Oshra, Rabbi Sela, Rabbi Weiss, Shlomo and Malki, Alfredo and Hadassa, our Kehilat Kinor David. And a big thank-you to all of you present, including my friends Israel and Oded. Employment is an important thing – you gave me a job. You have never hesitated to help us.

"Thanks to all of you, I can see the good things in this Land and this beautiful people, a holy nation that we had the great privilege to join.

"May we be found worthy of this privilege.

"Thanks again for making this day very special."

Ruth does not regard herself as a public speaker. On our wedding day she surprised many of us by giving the following speech.

"Dear guests, I want to take this opportunity to thank you all for coming. Thank you Kinor David for making this day so wonderful for us. You have done more than enough. I also want to thank our dear friends Hadassa and Alfredo. Your home makes a perfect setting for a wedding.

"Hadassa, your warm personality is an inspiration, Alfredo, your intelligence is unique. How unique, you ask? I will tell you.

"Once we were sitting at your Shabbat table, as we have done so many times. Shlomo and I mentioned a campaign we heard about already in Finland. It was a Christian campaign in America with the slogan, 'We found it.' Not long after came the answer from the Jewish side with the slogan,

'We never lost it.' We thought it was a brilliant answer. How happy and surprised we were to find out that the source and idea came from Alfredo and his Jewish students in the States.

"In our case today we can say: We found what you never lost.

"For Shlomo and me, today is not just a wedding. It is a completion. Ten years have passed since we started on our road towards Judaism, so we have had ample time to change our minds if we wanted to. One can say that our past religion is a very easy religion. A Christian Arab said in an interview a few weeks ago, 'I like being a Christian, it is the easiest religion and Christmas and Easter are really nice holidays.'

"If Christianity is the easiest religion, Judaism must be the hardest one. But we joined the Jewish faith, for better or for worse. When we met our *shaliach* in Helsinki before our departure to Israel, she said, 'the first year in Israel will be like hell, but after that it will be paradise' – I wish she was right. In any case, here is the only place where Israel can be a nation.

"Rambam established the fundamental halachic ruling that living in Israel is a commandment of the Torah. We are commanded to conquer and settle the land. This applies to every generation and every Jew. I love the writings of Rabbi Kook, especially his writings about *Eretz Yisrael*. He says 'The genuine keeping of the Torah is only in *Eretz Yisrael* and the soul of Israel is the Torah.' According to Rabbi Kook the setbacks we face in settling the land are only temporary.

"We see how the God of Israel is bringing His people back and for some reason we got the privilege of coming here too. We are here to build a new line of Jewish families. I am very grateful to our daughters who wanted to follow their crazy parents all the way.

"May Hashem, who gives us such a great joy today, together with all of you, help us grow in faith and knowledge.

"Thank you for celebrating with us. It is a celebration of Judaism at its very best."

EIGHTEEN

We Made It Home

AFTER THE WEDDING our daily life began to take on a more regular shape – if there is such a thing in Israel. We had completed the requirements for conversion. The time and effort we now spend learning and attending lectures are because we choose to do so, and not because we have to review for an upcoming test. When life is hectic, demanding, and full of responsibilities, one's life philosophy is put to the test. One of Judaism's strengths, I have found, is the Shabbat. There is nothing more wonderful than seeing young people at the flower shop on Friday afternoon, buying a nice bouquet for their mother for her Shabbat table. The preparations always seem like a last-minute rush, but the effects are amazing. Traffic calms down, people walk in different directions, everybody to their own *Beit Knesset*. After the grind of the working week comes the highlight of *Kabbalat Shabbat* and the Shabbat evening prayers. Then home to the beautifully-set Shabbat table. The wife has lit candles, the children have set the table, visitors are invited, all is prepared for *Kiddush*, the blessing recited over a cup of wine at the beginning of the Friday night meal. Suddenly you realize the miracle of Shabbat peace. Everybody greets you with "Shabbat Shalom," from Thursday morning onwards, at the shops, and then of course during Shabbat itself. No matter how hectic your week was, once you have recited *Kiddush*, and begun your Shabbat meal, the peace, calm, and quiet permeates the air. The family is together, all your worries are far away. The returning moment of Shabbat in the life of a Jew, week after week, is the battery charger for body and soul.

We left our homeland and our families and came to live with a people we had not known before, to find refuge under the wings of Hashem. We made *aliyah* to *Am Yisrael* and to *Eretz Yisrael*. My soul is at peace as a Jew, and every step I take on the soil of Israel is a source of joy. My mind, heart, and soul are humble and grateful that the God of Israel heard our prayers and accepted me and my family as His own, brought us to His Land and planted us here for future generations.

A pull is gentler than a push. It is better to be pulled to *Eretz Yisrael* than pushed out of the land of exile. Listen to the pull from the Holy Land. The whispering is calling you to come home. The Land of Israel is a gift to every Jew; it belongs to you and to your children.

Hear O Israel: The Lord our God, the Lord is One.

שמע ישראל יהוה אלוהינו יהוה אחד

You can contact the author by emailing him at: brunell@bezeqint.net or srb5396@yahoo.com.

Afterwords

DURING THE TIME that elapsed between finishing the manuscript and finalizing the editing of this book, we celebrated some enjoyable events in the family. One of our daughters, Karolin, got married. We witnessed an almost miraculous showering of helpfulness and joy from our wonderful community of friends. But there was more to the events surrounding the wedding than the memorable evening of the 11th of *Av*, July 2004. My wife Ruth started to remember the wording of her prayers back in Finland before the commencement of our conversion or *aliyah* preparations. Luckily we never lost our faith although we lived through a phase, after leaving the church, when we were not members of any religion. We still had our faith, however, and we had a God whom we prayed to. Ruth used to beg in her prayers that we would be granted the privilege of becoming one with the Jewish people. Without any doubt we had already rejoiced over the answer to this prayer when we passed the conversion process and were allowed to make *aliyah*. But in the events leading up to the wedding we realized that there were even deeper answers to our prayers that were about to be fulfilled.

Karolin had met her husband-to-be, Josef Polak. A year later he proposed and we met the entire Polak family at the engagement party. Meeting Josef's grandmother Frida, a Holocaust survivor, made us realize that our family is about to expand into families and generations dating back to "our forefathers." We were certainly becoming united with the Jewish nation.

As a tribute to the young couple that have given us so much joy, I want to end with the words I spoke at the wedding:

It is my great pleasure tonight to welcome you to the wedding of Karolin and Yossi. On behalf of my wife and I, I want to say a few words on this very special occasion. You are all included in this welcome, and I hope that you will enjoy this celebration with the Chatan and Kallah [bride and groom], the company at your table, the food and the music.

Thank you all, Holy Brothers and Sisters, for being here tonight and making this a beautiful reality. What a community – you are really speeding up the Geula [redemption]. Let me give a special welcome to our family from Finland and Sweden, my sister Berit and her husband Bengt, my brother Birger and his wife Benita, and Ruth's cousin Disa. You gave up the Scandinavian midnight sun for a week to come to the Gan Eden of Israel.

What a time for a wedding! Two days after Tisha BeAv [the ninth day of the Hebrew month of Av, which is a fast day]. The fasting will be gladly forgotten after this night. But life is much more than food and drink – believe it or not.

Looking back we might ask, why do we fast on Tisha BeAv? And why did the Chatan break a glass under the chuppah tonight? The answer is, because these two actions – fasting and breaking the glass - are connected. The questions relate to Jerusalem and to the missing Beit HaMikdash (The Temple). Because the first and second temples were destroyed on that day, the ninth of Av, we mourn their destruction, and we pray that the third and final Beit HaMikdash will be speedily rebuilt soon in our days. And what about such a happy occasion as tonight when a young couple is about to embark upon building their new home and future? Why do we need to connect this happiness to the destruction of Jerusalem by breaking a glass? I'd like to point to one answer. There are certainly many.

We must remember our roots, our connection to Am Yisrael; without the past there is no direction for the future. It's like a boat without a rudder – it cannot be maneuvered. Just as the rudder sits at the aft of the ship so does our history that is behind us guide our future, if we hold on to it.

I remember a long time ago, back in Finland, I used to have a small boat. I liked to go out fishing. To steer this boat I had to hold on to a long stick that connected directly to the rudder. If I let go, the boat slowly started to veer in the wrong direction.

The history of Am Yisrael has to be present at every occasion – whether it's for a sad or happy purpose – because it is a guarantor for the future. The history, i.e., the Holy Torah, is the rudder that can steer our life in the right direction and to the right goal. But we have to hold on to it like the skipper holds on to the rudder of his boat. We have to hold on to the Holy Torah with its infinite wisdom, not add to it, nor take away. This is a lesson stated clearly in this week's parsha (VaEtchanan), a Torah reading that includes both the Ten Commandments and the Shema. Our history does not whitewash defeats or mistakes – we have to learn from our mistakes and remember them. Therefore we fast and break the glass.

After the fasting, mourning, and breaking the glass in remembrance of the destroyed temple, we receive consolation: the disaster and disappointment is not the end, the city will be rebuilt, you will see bride and groom rejoice again, children dancing in the streets of Jerusalem (Zech 8:5). This is the message during the seven following weeks leading up to Rosh Hashana (Jewish New Year) and Yom Kippur.

God himself is the guarantor of our future in Eretz Yisrael. He says, "I, I am He Who consoles you" (Isaiah 51:12). He doesn't leave it up to our leaders or up to us. Baruch Hashem. We must do our share, but ultimately Hashem, the One and Only God of Israel, God of the Universe, will fulfill all the promises given to his people.

That's the guarantee for a good future, for the Chatan and Kallah, for all of Am Yisrael.

Dear Mr. and Mrs. Yossi Polak, you are so lucky tonight. The future is in good hands. And your future starts today. We wish you happiness, blessings, and many happy occasions to celebrate the beautiful life in Eretz Yisrael.

Dear Guests! I want you to know how much this means for my wife and me. After our entry into Am Yisrael and Eretz Yisrael, this step taken by the young couple, the brave and beautiful proposal by Yosef to our Karolin, this will graft us even more strongly and deeply into the family tree of Am Yisrael. What more can we wish!

Am Israel Chai. Mazal Tov! LeChaim!

Father of the Bride
Shlomo Brunell

A very happy occasion. At Karolin's and Yosef's wedding in 2004

Linda, Ruth, Karolin, Yosef Polak, Shlomo, Sara and Josefin